First published in Great Britain in 2017
by Wymer Publishing
www.wymerpublishing.co.uk
Tel: 01234 326691
Wymer Publishing is a trading name of Wymer (UK) Ltd

First edition. Copyright © 2017 Wymer Publishing.

**ISBN 978-1-908724-64-9**

The Author hereby asserts his rights to be identified
as the author of this work in accordance with sections
77 to 78 of the Copyright, Designs & Patents Act 1988.

All rights reserved. No part of this publication may be
reproduced or transmitted in any form or by any means,
electronic or mechanical, including photocopying, or any
information storage and retrieval system, without written
permission from the publisher.

This publication is sold subject to the condition that it shall not,
by way of trade or otherwise, be lent, re-sold, hired out or
otherwise circulated without the publishers prior consent in any
form of binding or cover other than that in which it is published
and without a similar condition including this condition
being imposed on the subsequent purchaser.

Every effort has been made to trace the copyright holders of the
photographs in this book but some were unreachable. We would
be grateful if the photographers concerned would contact us.

Typeset by Wymer.
Printed and bound in UK by Mixam.

A catalogue record for this book is available from the British Library.

Design by Wymer.
All images © Steve Emberton & Alan Perry.
Front cover photo © Steve Emberton.
Rear cover photos © Steve Emberton & Alan Perry.

# CONTENTS

*Preface*

**1.**
1976

**2.**
1977

**3.**
1978

**4.**
1979

**5.**
1980

**6.**
1981

# PREFACE

Everyone with an interest in Punk will have their own opinion as to its origins; who were the truly defining bands, when it really started or when Punk morphed in to New Wave. Or even if it did at all?

We can all argue until we are blue in the face. Who were the best, who were just charlatans or even who were just using it as a springboard to a career. But does it really matter? There is no doubt that 1976 and '77 were the defining years for the Punk movement in Britain and the wealth of new bands that came along and changed the face of the music scene are a testimony to that. Was it a direct consequence of the landscape that the youth found themselves in, in the late seventies?

As one of those who was a teenager when the Sex Pistols, The Stranglers, The Clash etc emerged was I any more rebellious than the generation before me? The Mods and Rockers of the sixties, or the Teddy boys of the fifties? Was the music anymore anarchic?

Once again these are questions we can all pontificate on but what the hell. Does it really matter? What Punk certainly had, just as Elvis and Jerry Lee Lewis had twenty years before it, or The Who and The Stones, in the following decade, was that elusive element that excites. That to me is really how music should be viewed. If it turns you on, it's got to be good.

This book is unlikely to turn you on as much as the first time you heard the Pistols, or went to a Damned gig, or whatever it might have been but hopefully it will bring back lots of happy memories for those who grew up during the period it covers.

Like any form of music, it never dies; it just changes and evolves. Sure, there aren't so many kids on the streets these days with spiky hair and safety pins in their clothing and there certainly aren't the same levels of controversy but you wouldn't be reading this if you didn't still have an interest in all that went on back then.

Indeed, young kids today, influenced by their parents or discovering Punk for the first time through social media will hopefully enjoy this read as much as the nostalgic middle aged folk that some of us now are!

I wanted to try and paint a picture of the late seventies and indeed early eighties in timeline form. Nothing original there I know, but I have thrown in all manner of events of the day, political, social, sporting and more, alongside events involving the music of the period. It is deliberately random and scattered. So if you read through this and think to yourself I can't believe this or that was overlooked, you can fill in the missing pieces to suit your own memories and hopefully there will be enough here to do that.

For the younger ones amongst you, those other events may help to place some context as to what was happening around the music that was blasting out from kids bedrooms, or perhaps a cassette player in some adolescent's Ford Cortina.

Choosing to elect the timeline style requires lots of research and verifying of dates. The toughest element of that is with record release dates. So much information I came up with was clearly wrong. All new records were released on Fridays yet various sources often gave different days of the week. I knew they were wrong and in some cases have gone for the nearest Friday to the dates discovered. Some are still bound to be wrong and for that I make no apology. I've done my best and don't get too hung up if you spot a few errors where that is concerned.

Primarily I hope this book takes you on a journey and if at the end of it, you are compelled to dig out some of those old 45s or albums and give them another spin then I will take that as mission accomplished. Come what may, the pages that follow will take you back in some shape or form to when Punk rocked.

*Andy Francis*

**MONDAY**

**05**

JANUARY

Ten Protestant men are killed in the Kingsmill massacre at South Armagh, Northern Ireland, by members of the Provisional Irish Republican Army, using the alias "South Armagh Republican Action Force".

THURSDAY

**29**

JANUARY

Twelve Provisional Irish Republican Army bombs explode in London's West End.

**FRIDAY**

**06**

**FEBRUARY**

Eddie And The Hot Rods release debut single 'Writing On The Wall' b/w 'Cruisin' In The Lincoln.

**THURSDAY**

**12**

**FEBRUARY**

The Sex Pistols first public London date supporting Eddie & The Hot Rods at the Marquee.
The NME reports:

*A chair flies through the air, hitting the P.A system with a noise indistinguishable from the sound emanating from it. The chair was thrown by singer Johnny Rotten. But it's impossible to tell whether he'd thrown it in anger or excitement. The Pistols have played less than a dozen gigs so far, but they've already built up a fanatical teenage following. They play Small Faces numbers, early Kinks B-sides, a couple of Stooges tracks and only a handful of their own songs. "Actually we're not into music," says one of the group afterwards. "We're into chaos."*

Hot Rods; guitarist Dave Higgs said, "They can't play or nuffink. They just insult the audience. They wrecked our PA. We waited for them to apologise, but they had fucked off."

### Don't look over your shoulder, but the Sex Pistols are coming

**Sex Pistols**
**MARQUEE**

"HURRY UP, they're having an orgy on stage," said the bloke on the door as he tore the tickets up.
I waded to the front and staightway sighted a chair arcing gracefully through the air, skidding across the stage and thudding contentedly into the PA system, to the obvious nonchalance of the bass drums and guitar.
Well I didn't think they sounded *that* bad on first earful — then I saw it was the singer wh'd done the throwing.
He was stalking round the front rows, apparently scuffing over the litter on the floor between baring his teeth at the audience and stopping to chat to members of the group's retinue. He's called Johnny Rotten and the moniker fits.
Sex Pistols? Seems I'd missed the cavortings with the two scantily clad (plastic thigh boots and bodices) pieces dancing up front. In fact, I only caught the last few numbers; enough, as it happens, to get the idea. Which is ... a quarter of spiky teenage misfits from the wrong end of various London roads, playing 60's styled white punk rock as unself-consciously as it's possible to play it these days i.e. self-consciously.
Punks? Springsteen Bruce and the rest of 'em would get shredded if they went up against these boys. They've played less than a dozen gigs as yet, have a small but fanatic following, and don't get asked back. Next month they play the Institute of Contemporary Arts if that's a clue.
I'm told the Pistols repertoire includes lesser known Dave Berry and Small Faces numbers (check out early Kinks' B-sides leads), besides an Iggy and the Stooges item and several self-penned numbers like the moronic "I'm Pretty Vacant," a meandering power-chord job that produced the chair-throwing incident.

No-one asked for an encore but they did one anyway: "We're going to play 'Substitute'."
"You can't play," heckled an irate French punter.
"So what?" countered the bassman, jutting his chin in the direction of the bewildered Frog.

That's how it is with the Pistols — a musical experience with the emphasis on Experience.
"Actually, we're not into music," one of the Pistols confided afterwards.
"Wot then?"
"We're into chaos."
— Neil Spencer

*Pistols' Johnny Rotten: it fits.*

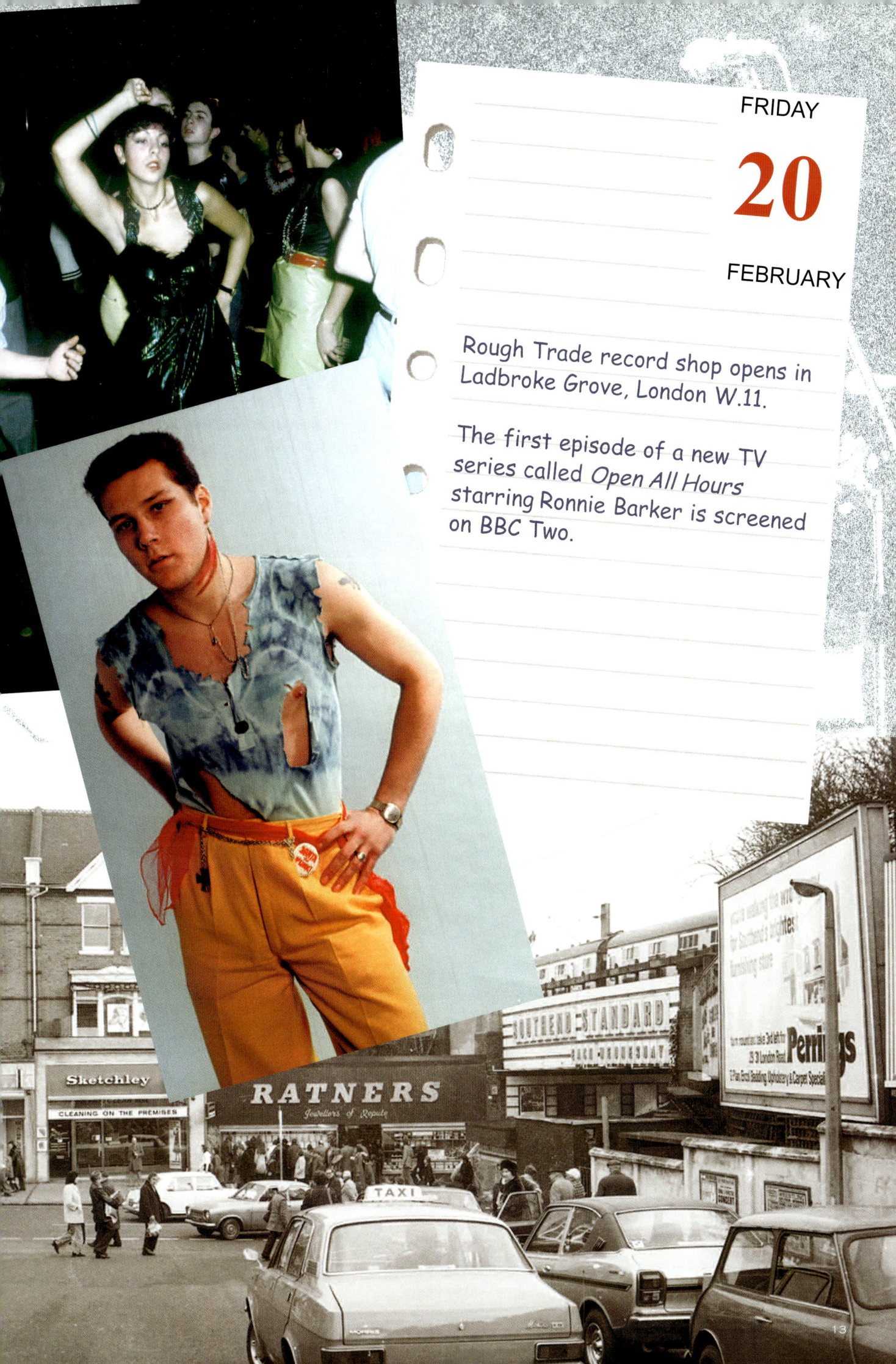

FRIDAY
20
FEBRUARY

Rough Trade record shop opens in Ladbroke Grove, London W.11.

The first episode of a new TV series called Open All Hours starring Ronnie Barker is screened on BBC Two.

**SUNDAY**
**07**
MARCH

The Stranglers play Hornsey Art College in London supported by The Vibrators playing their first gig.

**TUESDAY**
**16**
MARCH

Prime Minister Harold Wilson resigns after 13 years as Labour leader and nearly eight as First Lord of the Treasury.

## MONDAY
## 05
### APRIL

James Callaghan is elected Labour Party leader and becomes the new Prime Minister.

## WEDNESDAY
## 07
### APRIL

Cabinet minister John Stonehouse resigns from the Labour Party leaving the Government without a majority in the House of Commons.

**FRIDAY**

# 23

APRIL

The Sex Pistols appear at the Nashville, London. A fight breaks out prompting a mini-feature in the *New Musical Express*.

The Ramones release their eponymous titled debut studio album *Ramones*.

Also this month:
Stiff Records is created in London with an ideal of signing almost exclusively punk and punk-inspired musicians.

**MONDAY**

**10**

MAY

Jeremy Thorpe resigns as leader of the Liberal Party.

**TUESDAY**

**11**

MAY

The Sex Pistols begin a residency at London's 100 Club.

**SUNDAY**

**16**

MAY

Patti Smith's British debut at The Roundhouse, supported by The Stranglers.

THURSDAY

## 20

MAY

The Sex Pistols record a session with guitarist/producer Chris Spedding.

THURSDAY

## 27

MAY

The Stranglers play Brunel University in Uxbridge with support act The Jam.

**TUESDAY**

**01**

JUNE

Britain and Iceland end their Cod War with a compromise, an agreement allowing a maximum of 24 British fishing boats within 200 miles of Iceland.

**THURSDAY**

**17**

JUNE

Kilburn and The High Roads, The Sex Pistols and The Stranglers play at the Assembly Hall Walthamstow.

**TUESDAY**

**22**

JUNE

Heat wave reaches its peak with the temperature attaining 26.7 °C (80 °F).

**SATURDAY**

# 03

JULY

Heat wave peaks with temperatures reaching 35.9 °C (96.6 °F) in Cheltenham.

20-year old Swede Bjorn Borg becomes the youngest Wimbledon champion of the modern era when he beats the favoured Illie Nastase in straight sets.

**SUNDAY**

# 04

JULY

The Ramones first non-US appearance supporting Flamin' Groovies at London's Roundhouse with The Stranglers third on the bill.

The Sex Pistols play the Black Swan pub in Sheffield with support act The Clash.

## MONDAY 05 JULY

Flamin' Groovies, The Ramones and The Stranglers play at Dingwalls. Stranglers' bassist Jean-Jacques Burnel has a fight with Paul Simonon of The Clash.

## TUESDAY 06 JULY

The Sex Pistols play at the 100 Club supported by a new band The Damned.

## WEDNESDAY 07 JULY

David Steel is elected as the new leader of the Liberal Party.

## MONDAY 12 JULY

Kilburn & The High Roads featuring Ian Dury disband due to lack of success.

## SLAUGHTER & THE DOGS
### PRESENTED BY R. & B.
## THE SEX PISTOLS
### PRESENTED BY MALCOLM McLAREN
### PLUS SUPPORT
## TUES. 20th JULY 1976
### from 7.30 p.m.
### TICKETS £1.00
obtainable from the Box Office, or pay at the door.

---

**TUESDAY**

# 13
## JULY

Issue 1 of *Sniffin' Glue*, the first punk fanzine is published.

The Stranglers start a five-night stint at the Hope And Anchor in North London.

---

**TUESDAY**

# 20
## JULY

The Buzzcocks debut as support to The Sex Pistols at Manchester's Lower Free Trade Hall.

**FRIDAY**

**06**

AUGUST

The last person to serve as Postmaster General, John Stonehouse, is sentenced to seven years in gaol for fraud.

**FRIDAY**

**13**

AUGUST

The Clash play their first gig in London in Camden Town to a privately invited audience.

**SUNDAY**

**29**

AUGUST

Screen on the Green in Islington hosts a Midnight Special featuring The Sex Pistols, supported by the Clash and the Buzzcocks.

**MONDAY**

**30**

AUGUST

100 police officers and 60 carnival-goers are injured during riots at the Notting Hill Carnival.

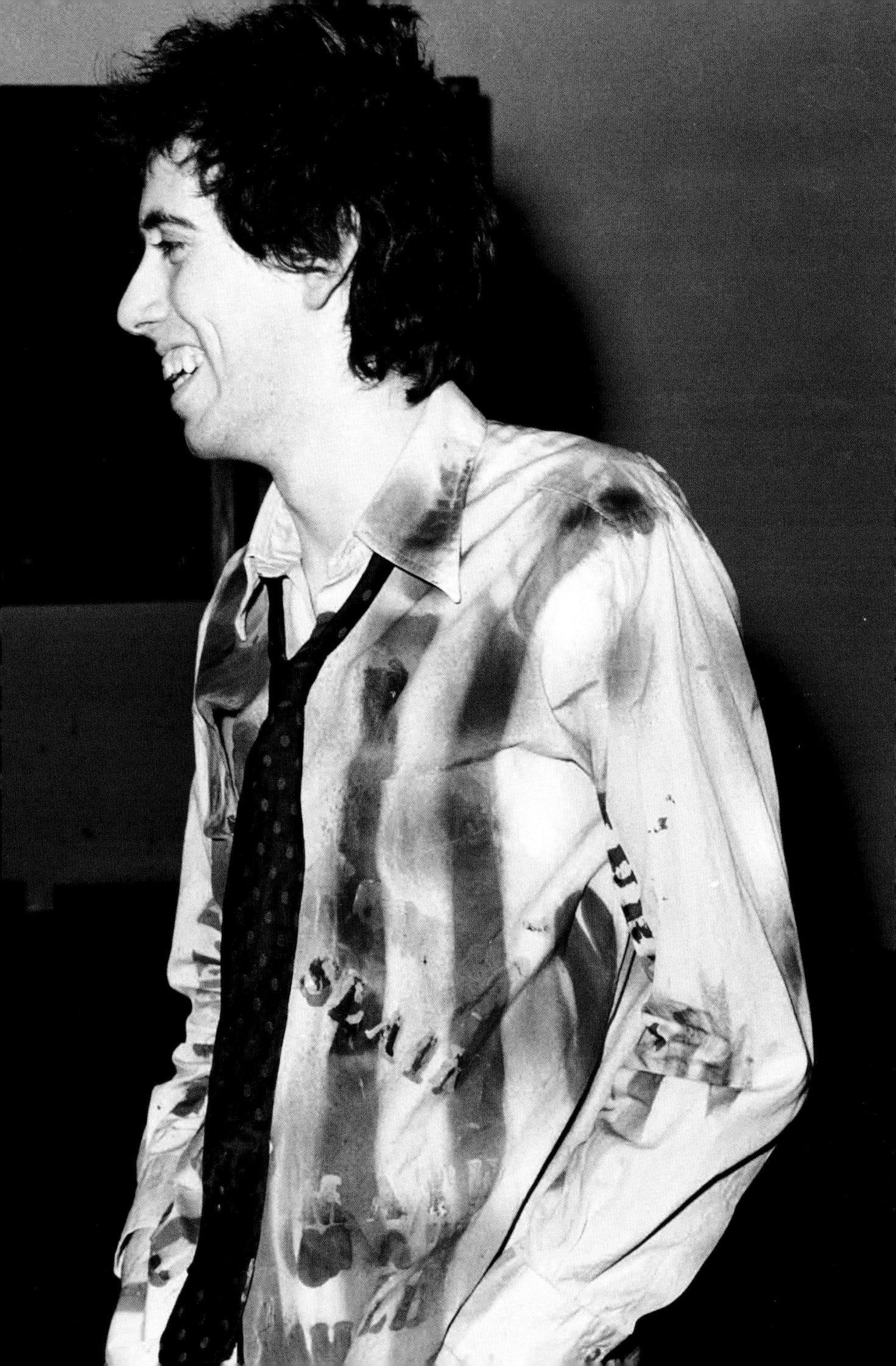

**MONDAY**

**20**

SEPTEMBER

A two-day punk festival organised by Malcolm McLaren begins at The 100 Club, London shows included: Subway Sect, Siouxsie & the Banshees, The Clash, The Sex Pistols, The Vibrators, The Damned, The Stinky Toys and Buzzcocks.

The Banshees improvised music as Siouxsie sang the 'Lord's Prayer'. The performance lasted 20 minutes.

**SATURDAY**

**09**

OCTOBER

The Sex Pistols sign to EMI for £40,000. "Here at last is a group with a bit of guts for younger people to identify with," says a spokesman.

**FRIDAY**

**22**

OCTOBER

The Damned release 'New Rose', the first single marketed as "punk rock".

**SUNDAY**

# 07

**NOVEMBER**

The Stranglers play The Marquee Club with Ducks Deluxe but are banned from playing the venue in future after Jean-Jacques Burnel puts his boot through a window.

**FRIDAY**

# 19

**NOVEMBER**

Eddie & The Hot Rods release debut album, *Teenage Depression*. Michael Beal's cover art is of a young man holding a gun to his head.

The Vibrators first release is actually two singles released by RAK on the same day. The first is 'We Vibrate' and the second is 'Pogo Dancing' by Chris Spedding and The Vibrators.

**SUNDAY**

## 21

**NOVEMBER**

Billy Idol plays his last gig with Chelsea before leaving to form Generation X.

**FRIDAY**

## 26

**NOVEMBER**

Sex Pistols release 'Anarchy In The U.K.' on EMI.

**WEDNESDAY**

## 01

**DECEMBER**

Sex Pistols and members of the Bromley Contingent (including Banshees Siouxsie Sioux & Steve Severin) appear live on *Today* show on ITV.
Host Bill Grundy shows an interest in Siouxsie and the band unleashes a torrent of expletives.

**THURSDAY**

## 02

**DECEMBER**

Daily Mirror runs the headline "The Filth And The Fury!" A reaction to the *Today* show interview.

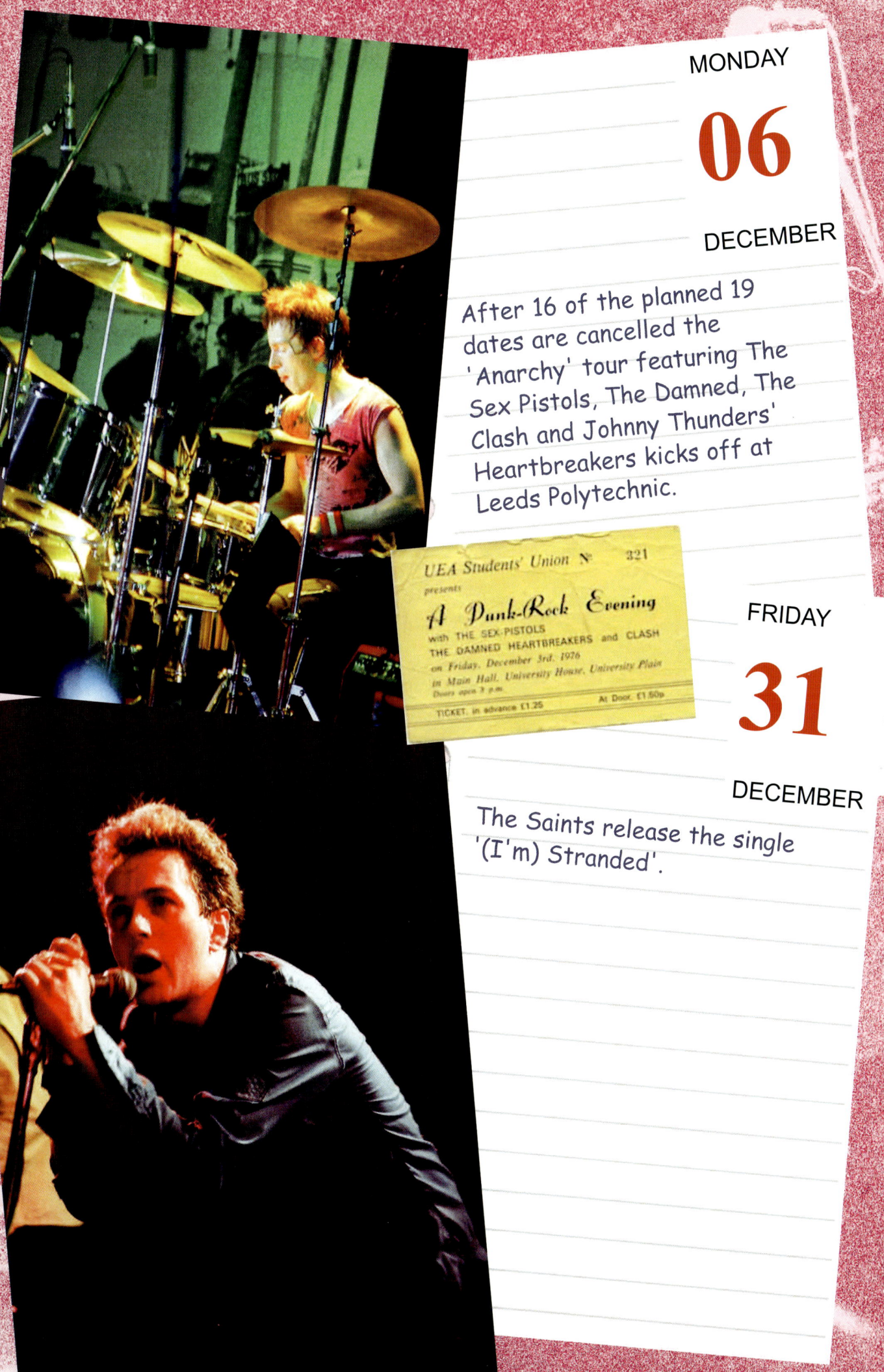

**MONDAY**

**06**

DECEMBER

After 16 of the planned 19 dates are cancelled the 'Anarchy' tour featuring The Sex Pistols, The Damned, The Clash and Johnny Thunders' Heartbreakers kicks off at Leeds Polytechnic.

**FRIDAY**

**31**

DECEMBER

The Saints release the single '(I'm) Stranded'.

**SATURDAY**

# 01

## JANUARY

Andy Czezowski opens The Roxy venue in London's Covent Garden. The Clash & The Heartbreakers performs on the opening night.

**THURSDAY**

# 06

## JANUARY

EMI sacks the Sex Pistols for their behaviour on ITV's Today Show, whose presenter Bill Grundy was also dismissed by his employers for inciting them.

## FRIDAY 28 JANUARY

'(Get A) Grip (On Yourself)' by The Stranglers is released.

Buzzcocks's release their debut *Spiral Scratch* EP single on their independent label New Hormones.

Seven Provisional Irish Republican Army bombs explode in the West End of London, but there are no fatalities or serious injuries.

EMI Records agree a financial settlement with The Sex Pistols of £30,000 on top of their advance.

## SATURDAY 30 JANUARY

The Stranglers' Hugh Cornwell gets into bother with the Greater London Council for wearing a t-shirt on stage at the Rainbow Theatre with the word fuck in the style of the Ford Motor Company logo.

---

**THE ROXY CLUB.**
41-43 NEAL ST., LONDON W.C.2

OPEN EVERY NIGHT EXCEPT FRIDAYS DURING JANUARY. FROM FEB 1ST OPEN 7 NIGHTS A WEEK. FREE MEMBERSHIP.

*Sniffin' Glue JAN 77*

DATES:
MON 17TH JAN - DAMNED/BOYS.
WED 19TH JAN - SLAUGHTER + THE DOGS/ADVERTS.
THURS 20TH JAN - SQUEEZE/ZIPS.
SAT 22ND JAN - STRANGLERS/A PLAY! WITH REAL ACTORS!
THURS 27TH JAN - VIBRATORS/OUTSIDERS.
SAT 29TH JAN - GENERATION X/?
MON 31ST JAN - DAMNED/REJECTS.

ADMISSION FEE VARIES. (NORMALLY - £1). FREE ADMISSION ON NON-GROUP NIGHTS DURING JAN.

**FRIDAY 18 FEBRUARY**

The debut album Damned Damned Damned by The Damned is released on Stiff Records. It is the first album released by a UK punk band. The album reaches No.36 UK, but fails to chart in the US.

**TUESDAY 22 FEBRUARY**

During a concert at Essex University, Colchester by The Stranglers and The Damned, Jean-Jacques Burnel receives a bottle to the head and needs three stitches.

**FRIDAY 25 FEBRUARY**

Polydor Records announce they have signed The Jam.

The Damned release 'Neat Neat Neat'.

**MONDAY 28 FEBRUARY**

Sid Vicious replaces Glen Matlock as the Sex Pistols bassist.

Also this month Howard Devoto leaves the Buzzcocks. Guitarist Pete Shelley becomes the vocalist.

| TUESDAY | |
|---|---|
| **01** | The Clash begin their White Riot tour in Guilford, supported by The Jam, Buzzcocks, The Slits and Subway Sect. After a dispute The Jam leave the tour later in the month. |
| MARCH | |

James Callaghan threatens to withdraw state aid to British Leyland unless it puts an end to strikes.

| WEDNESDAY | |
|---|---|
| **09** | A & M Records signs the Sex Pistols. |
| MARCH | |

| THURSDAY | |
|---|---|
| **10** | Malcolm McLaren re-stages the previous days contract signing in front of Buckingham Palace. |
| MARCH | |

| TUESDAY | |
|---|---|
| **15** | British Leyland managers announce intention to dismiss 40,000 toolmakers who have gone on strike at the company's |
| MARCH | |

Longbridge plant in Birmingham, action which is costing the state-owned carmaker more than £10million a week.

**FRIDAY**
# 18
Having signed to CBS The Clash release their first single, 'White Riot'

MARCH

**FRIDAY**
# 08
The Clash's debut album *The Clash* is released in the UK.

APRIL

**FRIDAY**
# 15
The Stranglers release their debut album *Rattus Norvegicus*. Initial copies included a free single, 'Peasant In The Big Shitty' / 'Choosey Susie'.

APRIL

## MONDAY
# 09
### MAY

A gig at London's Rainbow Theatre with The Clash, The Jam, Buzzcocks, The Prefects and Subway Sect resulted in 200 trashed seats.
As the NME described it, there was little other damage. In fact, as riots go, it was an orderly one.

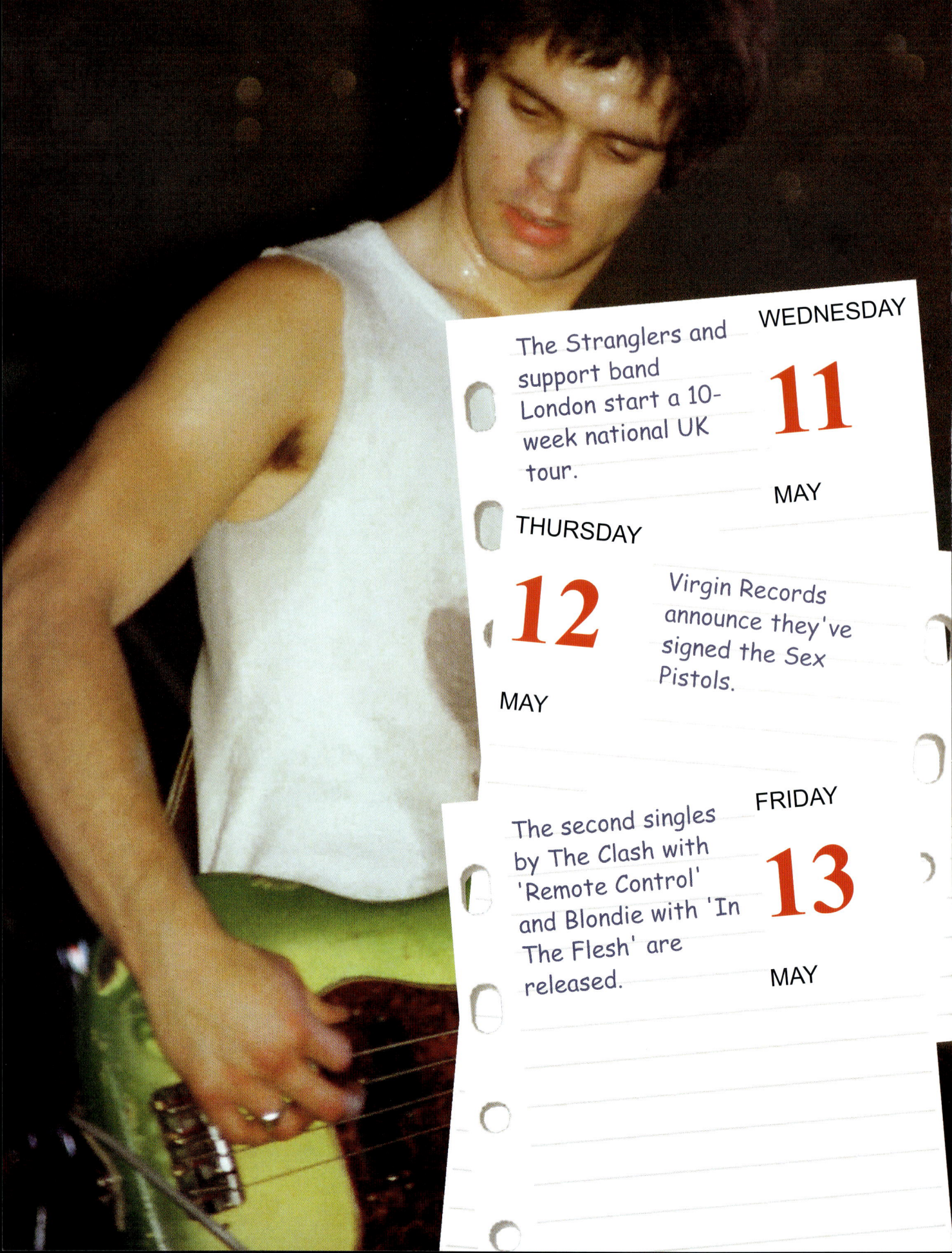

**WEDNESDAY 11 MAY**

The Stranglers and support band London start a 10-week national UK tour.

**THURSDAY 12 MAY**

Virgin Records announce they've signed the Sex Pistols.

**FRIDAY 13 MAY**

The second singles by The Clash with 'Remote Control' and Blondie with 'In The Flesh' are released.

**TUESDAY**

**17**

MAY

Elizabeth II commences her Jubilee tour in Glasgow.

**FRIDAY**

**20**

**MAY**

The Jam release their debut album *In The City*.

**FRIDAY**

**27**

**MAY**

Virgin releases The Sex Pistols' single 'God Save The Queen'.

**MONDAY**

**06**

**JUNE**

Three days of Jubilee celebrations commence to celebrate twenty-five years of Queen Elizabeth II's reign.

**TUESDAY**

**07**

**JUNE**

The Sex Pistols attempt to interrupt Silver Jubilee celebrations for Queen Elizabeth II by performing "God Save the Queen" from a rented boat to traverse down the River Thames. Police force them to dock, several Pistols fans are arrested and injured in the meleé. Among those arrested are Malcolm McLaren, Vivienne Westwood, artist Jamie Reid, Tracie O'Keefe and Debbie Juvenile of the Bromley Contingent.

43

**SATURDAY**

**18**

**JUNE**

During a break from a recording session Johnny Rotten, Chris Thomas (producer) and Bill Price (studio boss) are attacked outside the Pegasus pub. Johnny has his arm slashed open and suffers tendon damage.

**SATURDAY**

**25**

**JUNE**

Dublin stages its first all-day punk event at the Belfield Canteen billed as the 'Belfield Festival'. Headlining is The Radiators from Space. Other bands are: The Undertones, The Vipers, Revolver and The Gamblers. During the gig, a fight broke out and 18-year old student, Patrick Coultry is stabbed to death.

**THURSDAY**

**23**

**JUNE**

Johnny Rotten is attacked again, this time during a Pirate's gig at Dingwalls.

**SUNDAY**

**26**

**JUNE**

16-year-old shop assistant Jayne McDonald is found battered and stabbed to death in Chapeltown, Leeds; police believe she is the fifth person to be murdered by the Yorkshire Ripper.

Also this month: The Damned, The Stranglers and The Jam all have gigs cancelled and two members of The Clash are arrested after painting their names on a wall in London.

Singles released include 'Right To Work' by Chelsea, 'Fascist Dictator' by The Cortinas & 'Pure Mania' by The Vibrators.

*Yes, we know! But who is Celia?*

**Celia and the Mutations**

New Single Out Now
**Mony Mony**
c/w Mean To Me
UP 36262

UA

The Sex Pistols release 'Pretty Vacant', their first on the Virgin label.

**FRIDAY 01**
JULY

Jonathan King as Elizabeth releases 'God Save The Sex Pistols'.

**FRIDAY 08**
JULY

**SUNDAY**

**10**

JULY

Bradford woman Maureen Long, 42 is injured in an attack believed to have been committed by the Yorkshire Ripper in the West Yorkshire city.

**MONDAY**

**11**

JULY

Gay News found guilty of blasphemous libel in a case (Whitehouse v. Lemon) brought by Mary Whitehouse's National Viewers and Listeners Association.

**SATURDAY**

**16**

JULY

Johnny Rotten's first radio interview with Tommy Vance on Capital Radio is broadcasted. It's a 90 minute show called *A Punk and His Music*.

**FRIDAY**

**22**

JULY

The Stranglers release 'Something Better Change'.

**FRIDAY**

**29**

JULY

Eddie and the Hot Rods release 'Do Anything You Wanna Do'.

**SATURDAY**

**30**

JULY

The Sex Pistols begin their Scandinavian tour.

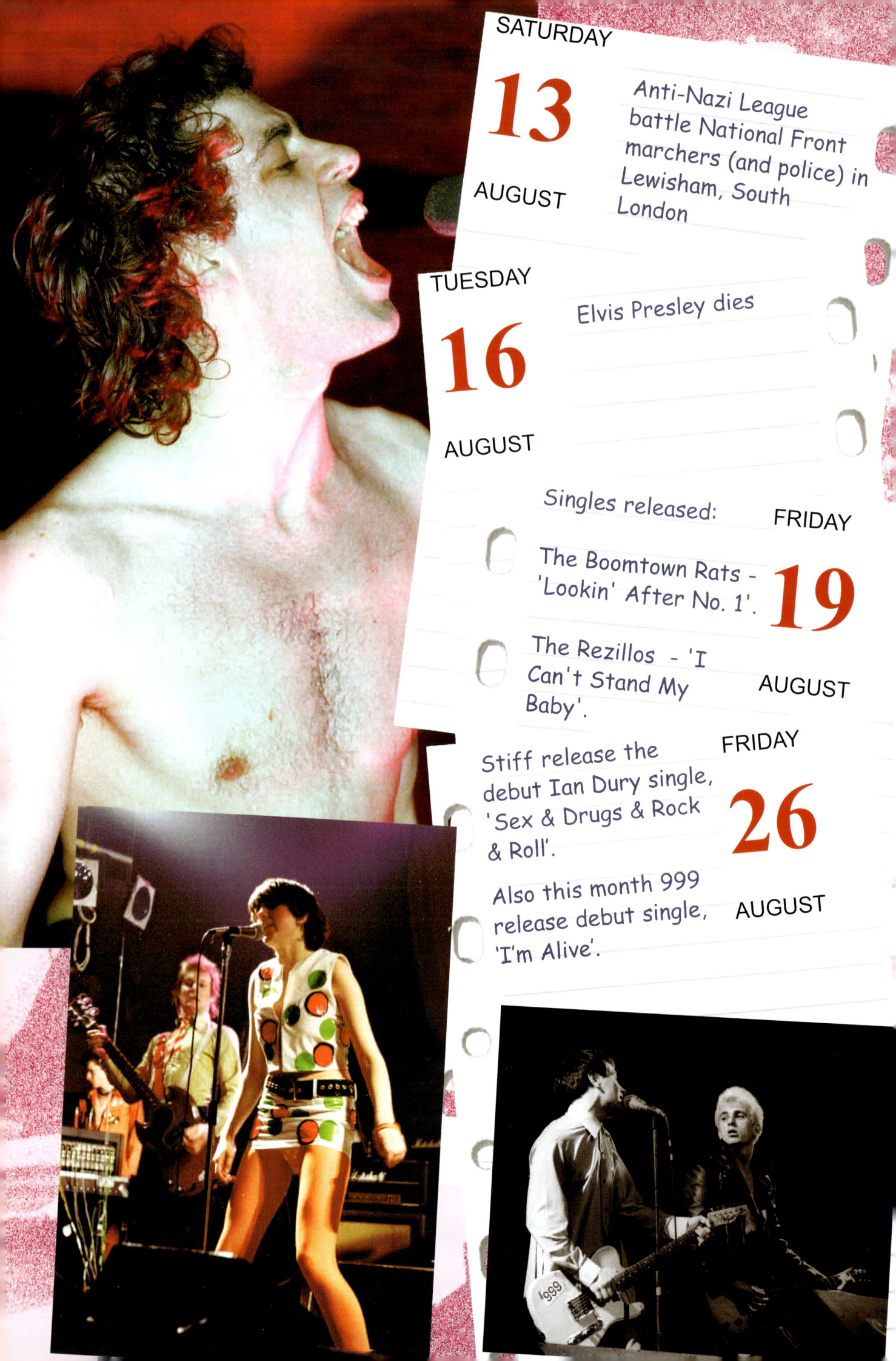

**SATURDAY**
**13**
AUGUST

Anti-Nazi League battle National Front marchers (and police) in Lewisham, South London

**TUESDAY**
**16**
AUGUST

Elvis Presley dies

**FRIDAY**
**19**
AUGUST

Singles released:
The Boomtown Rats - 'Lookin' After No. 1'.
The Rezillos - 'I Can't Stand My Baby'.

**FRIDAY**
**26**
AUGUST

Stiff release the debut Ian Dury single, 'Sex & Drugs & Rock & Roll'.
Also this month 999 release debut single, 'I'm Alive'.

**FRIDAY**
# 16
**SEPTEMBER**

Marc Bolan, glam rock pioneer at the start of the 1970s with T. Rex, is killed in a car crash in Barnes, London, two weeks before his 30th birthday. His girlfriend Gloria Jones, the driver of the car, is seriously injured. He'd just started his British comeback, touring with The Damned.

The Stranglers release 'No More Heroes'.

**SATURDAY**
# 17
**SEPTEMBER**

City Rock Festival, Chelmsford

The Rods, Doctors of Madness, The Damned, Chelsea, Slaughter and The Dogs, Fruit Eating Bears, Lew Lewis Band, Aswad, Glory, Solid Waste.

The Jam and Generation X had originally been billed but pulled out and The Damned didn't play.

## PUNK PROMOTERS GET ONE IN THE EYE

## Punk Flop: now who pays bills?

**FRIDAY**

# 23

**SEPTEMBER**

Jimmy Pursey arrested for playing on the roof of London's Vortex Club. He is fined £30.

'Complete Control' is released by The Clash.

Chelsea split.

**SUNDAY**

# 25

**SEPTEMBER**

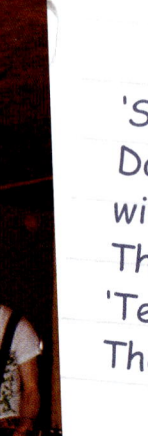

**FRIDAY**

# 30

**SEPTEMBER**

'Sounds journalists Giovanni Dadomo and Pete Makowski along with Steve Nicol from Eddie & The Hot Rods release the single 'Terminal Stupid' under the name, The Snivelling Shits.

Other single releases include: 'Oh Bondage Up Yours!' X-Ray Spex. New LPs include: New Boots and Panties!! by Ian Dury and the self-titled debut by The Boomtown Rats.

**MONDAY**
**10**
OCTOBER

Rat Scabies leaves The Damned.

**FRIDAY**
**14**
OCTOBER

The Sex Pistols release 'Holidays in the Sun'.

**THURSDAY**
**27**
OCTOBER

Former Liberal leader Jeremy Thorpe denies allegations of attempted murder of and having a relationship with male model Norman Scott.

**FRIDAY**
**28**
OCTOBER

Never Mind the Bollocks, Here's the Sex Pistols is released by Virgin Records. Despite refusal by major retailers to stock it, it debuts at number one on the UK Album Charts the week after its release.

**FRIDAY**
**04**
NOVEMBER

'Orgasm Addict' is released by The Buzzcocks.

**FRIDAY**
**11**
NOVEMBER

Singles released: 'Mary Of The 4th Form' (The Boomtown Rats)

'Don't Dictate' (Penetration)

**MONDAY**
**14**
NOVEMBER

Firefighters call their first ever national strike, demanding a 30% wage increase.

**FRIDAY**
**18**
NOVEMBER

The Jam release their second album, *This Is The Modern World*.

Richard Hell And The Voidoids release 'Blank Generation'.

**TUESDAY**
**22**
NOVEMBER

British Airways inaugurates regular London to New York City supersonic Concorde service.

**THURSDAY 01 DECEMBER**
Drugs squad raid the hotel room of Sid Vicious & Nancy Spungen.

**FRIDAY 02 DECEMBER**
'One Way Love' by The Damned and '(My Baby Does) Good Sculptures' by The Rezillos are released.

**SATURDAY 03 DECEMBER**
The England football team fails to achieve World Cup qualification for the second tournament in succession.

**WEDNESDAY 14 DECEMBER**
25-year-old Leeds prostitute Marilyn Moore is injured in an attack believed to have been committed by the Yorkshire Ripper.

**SUNDAY 18 DECEMBER**
Anne Beverley says: "My nickname for Sid's girlfriend is Nauseating Nancy".

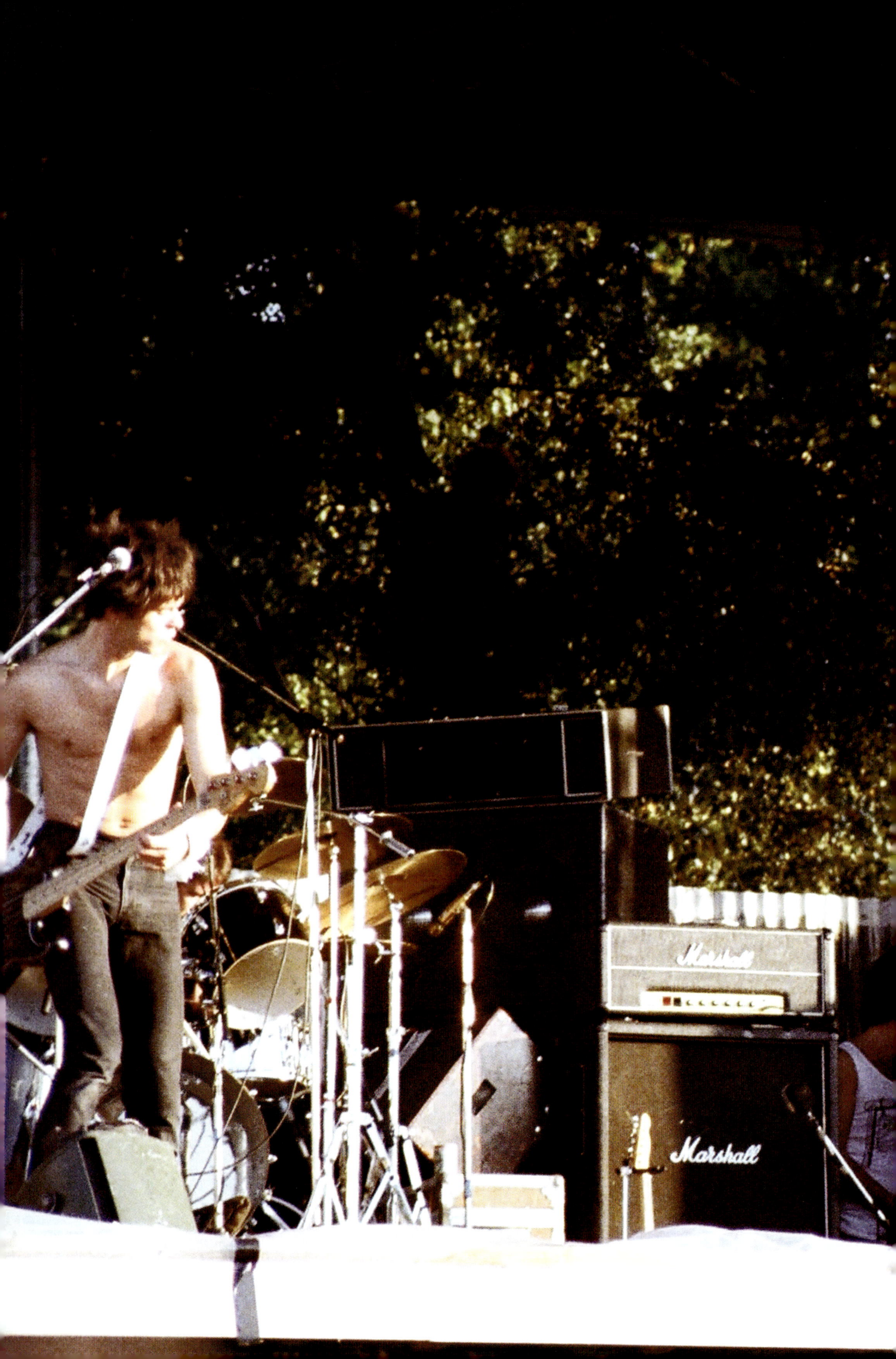
Marshall
Marshall

# 1978

**TUESDAY**
**05**
JANUARY

The Sex Pistols first US gig at the Great Southeast Music Hall, Atlanta, Georgia. Earlier gigs had been cancelled as initially they had been refused visa because of criminal convictions.

**TUESDAY**
**10**
JANUARY

Rough Trade refuses to stock the *Pretty Paedophiles* EP by Raped, describing it as "an insult to the women's movement".

**SATURDAY**
**14**
JANUARY

The Sex Pistols' disastrous January US tour ends. Johnny Rotten walks off stage at Winterland in San Francisco, famously uttering "Ever get the feeling you've been cheated?"

**THURSDAY**
**19**
JANUARY

The Sex Pistols split.

**WEDNESDAY**
**25**
JANUARY

Warsaw play first gig as Joy Division at Pip's Disco in Manchester.

**THURSDAY**
**26**
JANUARY

EMI refuses to press copies of Buzzcocks' 'Oh Shit'.

**FRIDAY**
**27**
JANUARY

The Stranglers release '5 Minutes'.

| SUNDAY | | TUESDAY | 18-year-old prostitute Helen Rytka is murdered in Huddersfield; she is believed to be the eighth victim of the Yorkshire Ripper. |
|---|---|---|---|
| **28** | Sham 69 begin their second national tour at the London School of Economics. | **31** | |
| JANUARY | | JANUARY | |

**FRIDAY**

**17**

**FEBRUARY**

The Clash release the single, 'Clash City Rockers'.

Debut albums by The Adverts (*Crossing the Red Sea with The Adverts*) and Sham 69 (*Tell Us The Truth*)

**WEDNESDAY**

**22**

**FEBRUARY**

Sid Vicious and Nancy Spungen arrested on charges of possessing dangerous drugs.

**TUESDAY**

**28**

**FEBRUARY**

The Damned break up.

Also this month: *Jubilee*, the cult punk-themed film directed by Derek Jarman premieres in London. It includes music by Adam Ant, Chelsea, Siouxsie and the Banshees, Wayne County and Toyah Willcox.

**THURSDAY**

**02**

MARCH

Chaplin's coffin is stolen from a Swiss cemetery.

**MONDAY**

**06**

MARCH

London's Vortex Club closed following damage caused during a UK Subs gig.

**FRIDAY**

**10**

MARCH

The Buzzcocks release the album, Another Music In A Different Kitchen and Wreckless Eric releases his self-titled debut album.

**THURSDAY**

**30**

MARCH

Paul Simonon and Topper Headon of The Clash arrested for shooting pigeons from the roof of their rehearsal

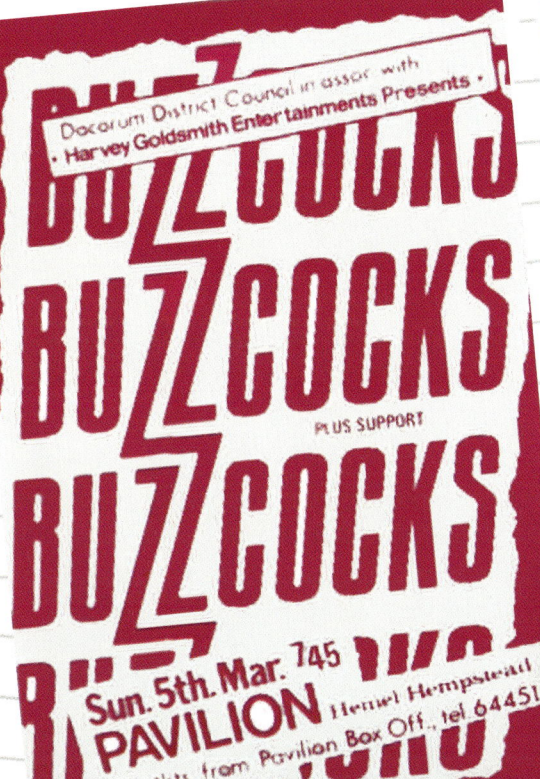

BUZZCOCKS
BUZZCOCKS
BUZZCOCKS
PLUS SUPPORT

Dacorum District Council in assoc with Harvey Goldsmith Entertainments Presents

Sun. 5th. Mar. 7.45
PAVILION Hemel Hempstead
adv tkts from Pavilion Box Off. tel 64451

**MONDAY**

**03**

**APRIL**

Permanent radio broadcasts of House of Commons proceedings begin.

**SATURDAY**

**22**

**APRIL**

Nottingham Forest win the Football League First Division title for the first time in their history under the guidance of manager Brian Clough.

**SUNDAY**

**30**

**APRIL**

Anti-Nazi League's carnival at Victoria Park, London attracts an 80,000 strong crowd.
The bill includes X Ray Spex, The Clash, Steel Pulse and the Tom Robinson Band.

Also this month The Vibrators release the album *V2* and The Skids release their debut single, 'Reasons'.

**SATURDAY**

**06**

A fan dies at a Vibrators gig at Preston after being injured in a fight between rival football fans.

MAY

**WEDNESDAY**

**10**

Paul Simonon and Topper Headon appear in court charged with criminal damage.

MAY

Liverpool F.C. retain the European Cup with a 1-0 win over Club Brugge K.V. at Wembley Stadium.

**FRIDAY**

**12**

The Stranglers release their third album, *Black and White*.

MAY

**WEDNESDAY**

**17**

Charlie Chaplin's coffin, stolen 11 weeks previous, is found in a field about a mile away from the Chaplin home in Corsier near Lausanne, Switzerland.

MAY

Also this month The Nipple Erectors release 'King Of The Bop' on Soho Records.

**FRIDAY**
**02**
JUNE

Joy Division release their debut EP, *An Ideal for Living*, on their own label.

**THURSDAY**
**08**
JUNE

Naomi James becomes the first woman to sail around the world single-handedly.

**FRIDAY**
**30**
JUNE

Steve Jones and Paul Cook, along with the Great Train Robber Ronnie Biggs release the *Biggest Blow* EP as the Sex Pistols.

Also this month The Lurkers release *Fulham Fallout*.

**TUESDAY**
**04**
JULY

Joe Strummer and Paul Simonon arrested in Glasgow for drunk and disorderly behaviour.

**WEDNESDAY**
**05**
JULY

Joe Strummer is fined £25 and Simonon £50 after being found guilty of breach of the peace.

**THURSDAY 13 JULY** — The BBC ban the Sex Pistols' 'No One Is Innocent'.

**FRIDAY 14 JULY** — Sham 69's 'If The Kids Are United' is released.

**RAR carnival**
JOHN COOPER-CLARKE has been added to the Manchester Rock Against Racism Carnival at Alexandra Park on July 13 and 15. Appearing with Graham Parker And The Rumour on the 15 will be the Fall (not the Fool as announced last week).

**SATURDAY 15 JULY** — Rock Against Racism's Northern Carnival in Alexandra Park, Manchester. Bill includes The Fall, Buzzcocks, John Cooper Clarke.

**WEDNESDAY 19 JULY** — 'No One Is Innocent' is banned by Capital Radio. Dead Kennedys play their first concert, at the Mabuhay Gardens in San Francisco, California.

**WEDNESDAY 23 AUGUST** — Jet Black fined £25 for breach of the peace in Glasgow.

Also this month Siouxsie and the Banshees' debut single 'Hong Kong Garden' is released.

**THURSDAY 07 SEPTEMBER** — Prime Minister James Callaghan announces that he will not call a general election for the autumn.

**SATURDAY 16 SEPTEMBER** — Strippers perform with the Stranglers during 'Nice 'N' Sleazy' at their Battersea Park gig.

**MONDAY 18 SEPTEMBER** — Rabid Records consult their lawyers after Pogo release a record by 'Gordon & Julie', characters created by Rabid artist Jilted John.

**THURSDAY 21 SEPTEMBER** — Sham 69 pull out of the Rock Against Racism gig because they don't want the blame for any trouble that might occur.

**SUNDAY 24 SEPTEMBER** — Rock Against Racism's massive Carnival is held in Brockwell Park, London.

**TUESDAY 26 SEPTEMBER** — 23 Ford car plants are closed across Britain due to strikes.

---

MUSIC MACHINE CAMDEN HIGH ST.
CHELSEA
THE FALL
THE SNIVELLING SHITS
8:00 MONDAY 25 SEPT

**THURSDAY**
**12**
OCTOBER

Nancy Spungen, found dead at New York's Hotel Chelsea (she died the previous day). Sid Vicious is charged with murder.

**FRIDAY**
**13**
OCTOBER

'Down In The Tube Station At Midnight' is released by The Jam.

**SUNDAY**
**15**
OCTOBER

Doctors of Madness split up.

**FRIDAY**
**27**
OCTOBER

Four people die and four others are wounded in a shooting spree which began in a residential street in West Bromwich and ends at a petrol station some 20 miles away in Nuneaton.

**SATURDAY**
**28**
OCTOBER

Barry Williams, aged 36, is arrested in Derbyshire and charged with the previous day's shootings following a high-speed police chase.

Also this month, Lene Lovich releases her debut album *Stateless*.

**SATURDAY**
**04**

Many British bakeries impose bread rationing after a baker's strike led to panic buying of bread.

NOVEMBER

'Germfree Adolescents' is released by X-Ray Spex.

**FRIDAY**
**10**

NOVEMBER

Paul Weller is accused of assault after an incident in a Leeds hotel.

**MONDAY**
**13**

NOVEMBER

**SUNDAY**
**19**

NOVEMBER

The Stranglers perform at University of Surrey in Guilford for BBC's Rock Goes To College. The BBC plans to start broadcasting after the first 4 songs. Because tickets had not been made available to regular fans but only university students. After performing the fifth song 'Hanging Around' Hugh Cornwell tells the audience to fuck off and the band walk off stage.

**THURSDAY**
**23**

NOVEMBER

Pollyanna's nightclub in Birmingham is forced to lift its ban on black and Chinese revellers, after a one-year investigation by the Commission for Racial Equality concludes that the nightclub's entry policy was racist.

**WEDNESDAY**

**29**

NOVEMBER

Viv Anderson, the 22-year-old Nottingham Forest defender, becomes England's first black international footballer in the 1-0 friendly win over Czechoslovakia at Wembley Stadium.

Also this month Siouxsie and the Banshees's debut album *The Scream* is released and Paul Weller is arrested for assault while staying at the same hotel as the Australian rugby league team.

**FRIDAY**

**01**

DECEMBER

Fay Fife & Eugene Reynolds split from The Rezillos.

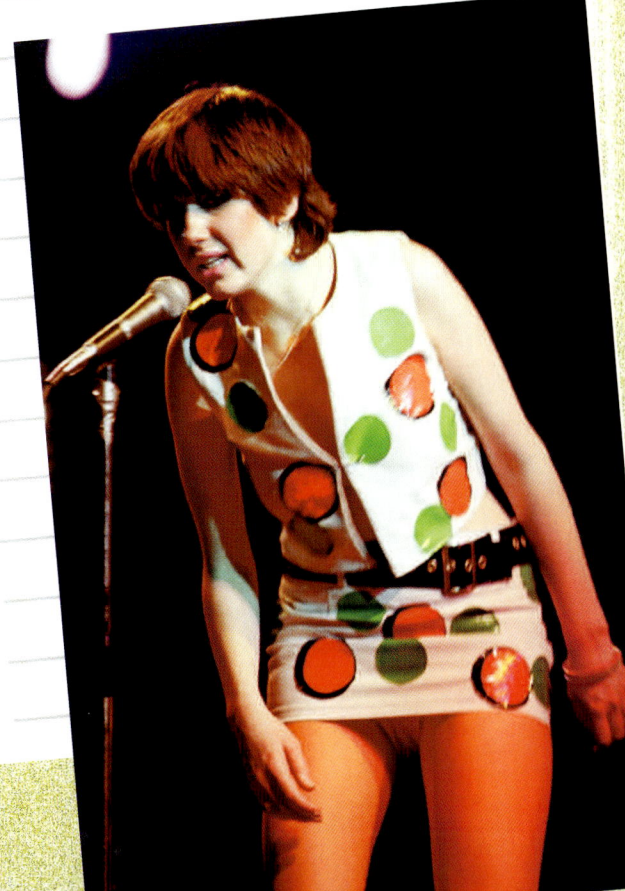

**FRIDAY**
**08**
DECEMBER

Public Image Ltd's eponymous debut album is released.

**THURSDAY**
**14**
DECEMBER

'Alternative Ulster' by Stiff Little Fingers tops *Sounds*' Alternative Chart.

**MONDAY**
**25**
DECEMBER

Public Image Ltd play their first live gig at the Rainbow Theatre.

Also this month, EMI releases the album *True Love Stories* by Graham Fellows under the name of Jilted John, following the success of the number 4 single 'Jilted John'.

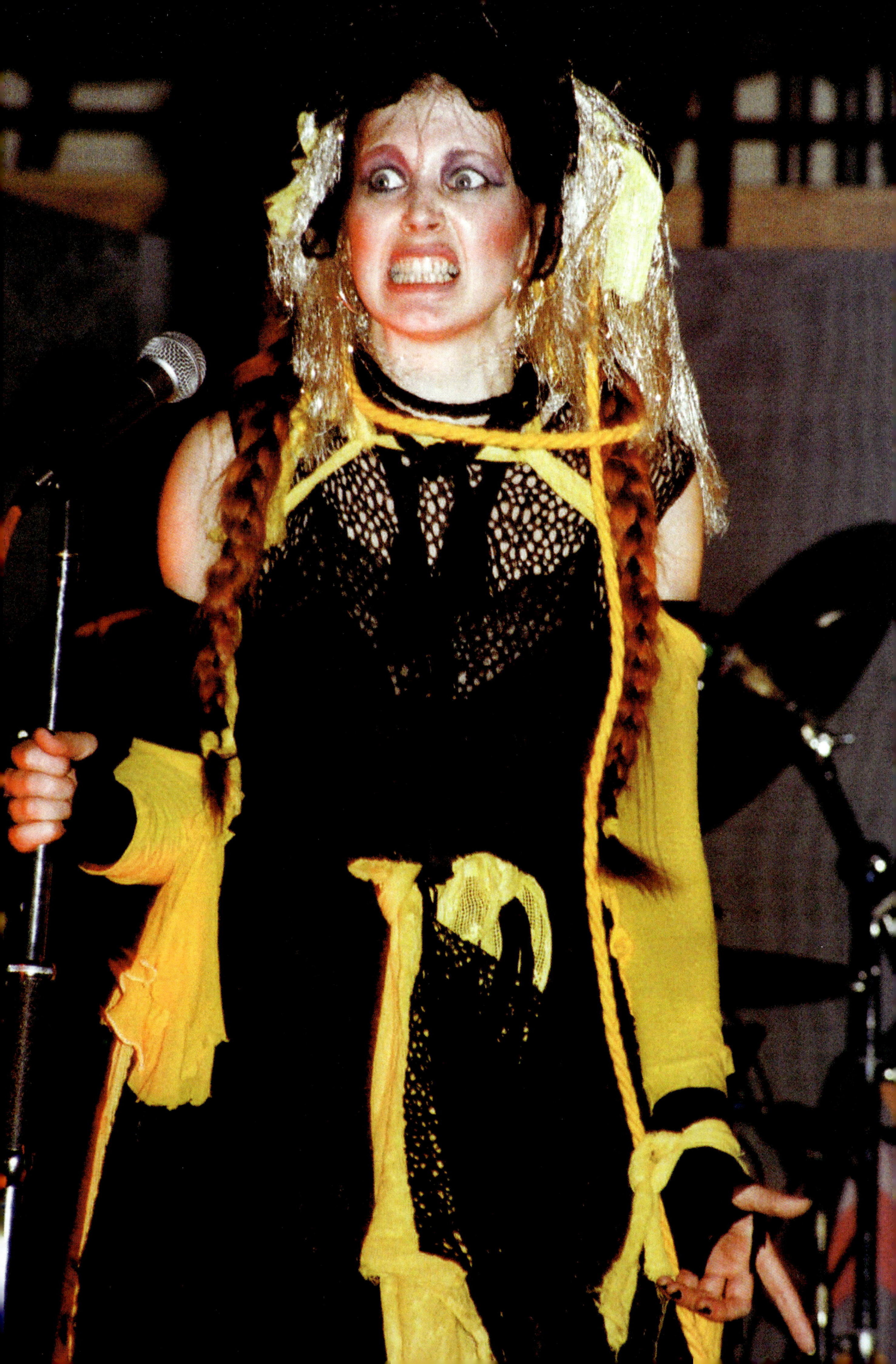

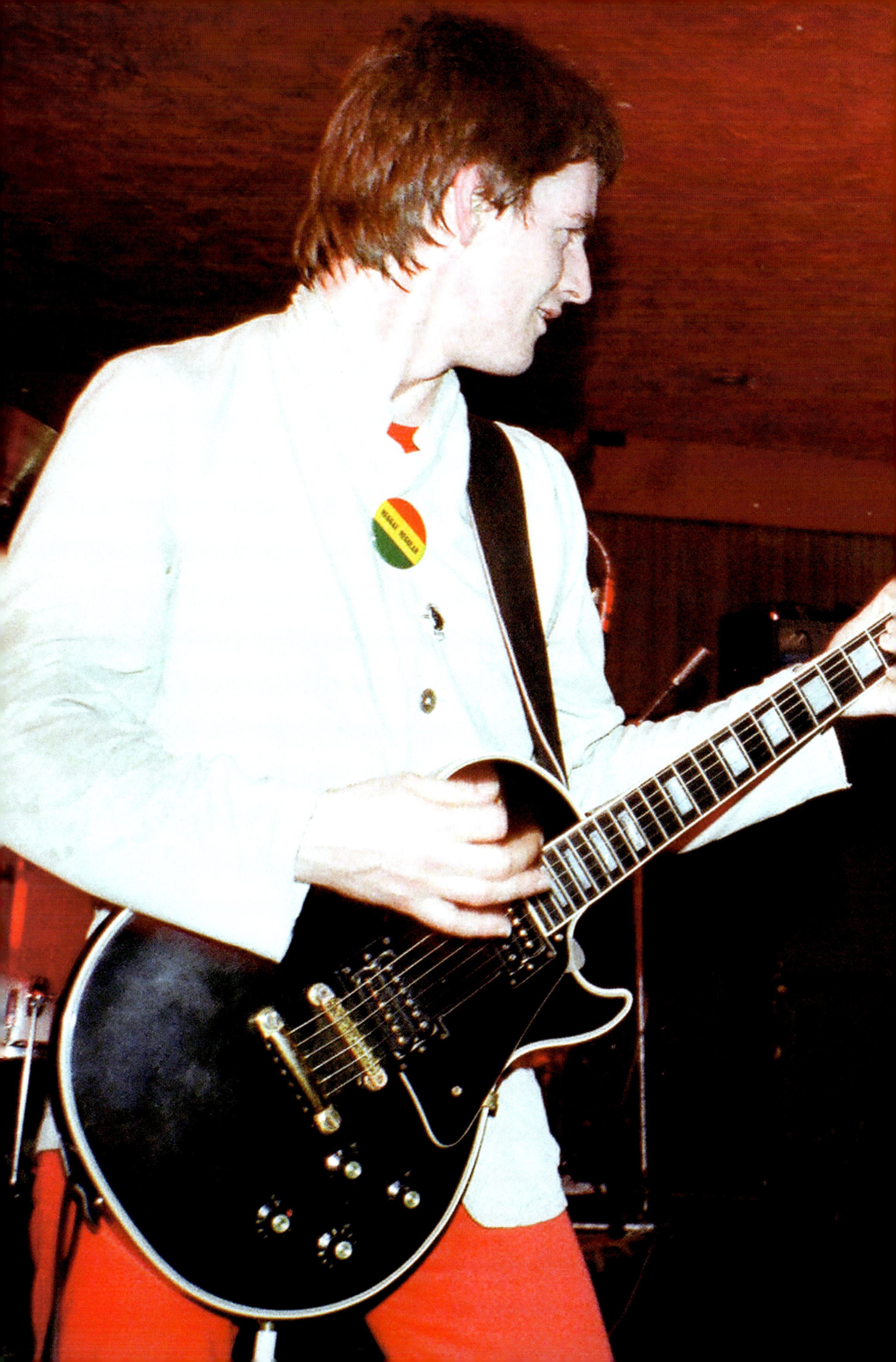

1979

**FRIDAY**

**12**

Time magazine names *Give 'Em Enough Rope* by The Clash as its album of the year for 1978.

**JANUARY**

**MONDAY**

**15**

Rail workers begin a 24-hour strike.

**JANUARY**

**MONDAY**

**22**

Tens of thousands of public-workers start strikes.

**JANUARY**

**FRIDAY**

**26**

Stiff release 'Lucky Number' by Lene Lovich.

**JANUARY**

**MONDAY**

**29**

JJ Burnel in the New Musical Express says "Rock 'n' Roll is about cocks and jiving and the odd bloody nose... and about people like us talking seriously about the social order."

**JANUARY**

NO FUTURE

FRIARS AT THE MAXWELL HALL AYLESBURY
SATURDAY, JANUARY 20th at 7.30pm
**THE LURKERS**
+ THE VICE CREEMS
+ THE STOWAWAYS
A C Sound and Vision
Tickets: 170p from Earth Records Aylesbury, Scorpion High Wycombe, Hairport Amersham, Old Town Records Hemel Hempstead, F.L. Moore Bletchley, Hi Vu Buckingham or 170p on door. Life membership 25p
Episode II in which Gerald & the man media believers turn on the heat.

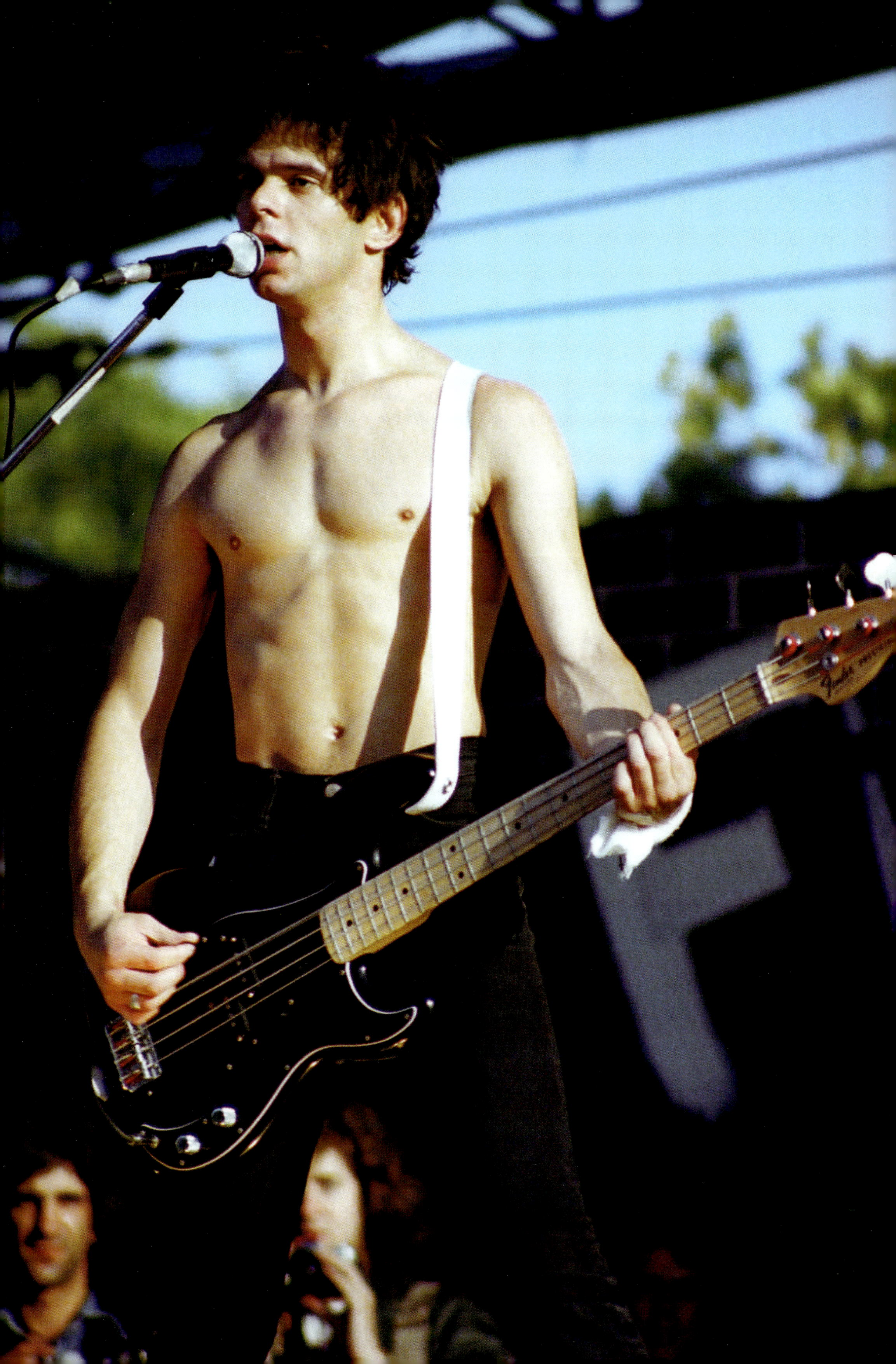
Fender

**THURSDAY 01 FEBRUARY**
Grave-diggers call off a strike in Liverpool which has delayed dozens of burials.

**FRIDAY 02 FEBRUARY**
Sid Vicious is found dead in New York after apparently suffocating on his own vomit as a result of a heroin overdose. He had been on bail charged with stabbing Nancy Spungen.

The Stranglers start a tour of Japan.

**MONDAY 12 FEBRUARY**
John Lydon's case against Malcolm McLaren over the Sex Pistols' earnings is adjourned.

Over 1,000 schools close due to the heating oil shortage caused by the lorry drivers' strike.

**WEDNESDAY 14 FEBRUARY**
The Clash play the Geary Theatre in San Fransisco.

**FRIDAY 16 FEBRUARY**
'Into The Valley' by The Skids is released.

**SATURDAY 17 FEBRUARY**
'Into The Valley' by The Skids is No.1 in the *Sounds* Alternative Chart.

**SUNDAY 18 FEBRUARY**
The BBC launches a new TV series, *Antiques Roadshow* in which specialists travel to various regions to appraise antiques brought in by local people.

**FRIDAY 23 FEBRUARY**
The Clash release 'English Civil War (Johnny Comes Marching Home)'.

**MONDAY 26 FEBRUARY**
It was revealed in court that only £30,000 remained of a total of £800,000 earned by the Sex Pistols since 1976.

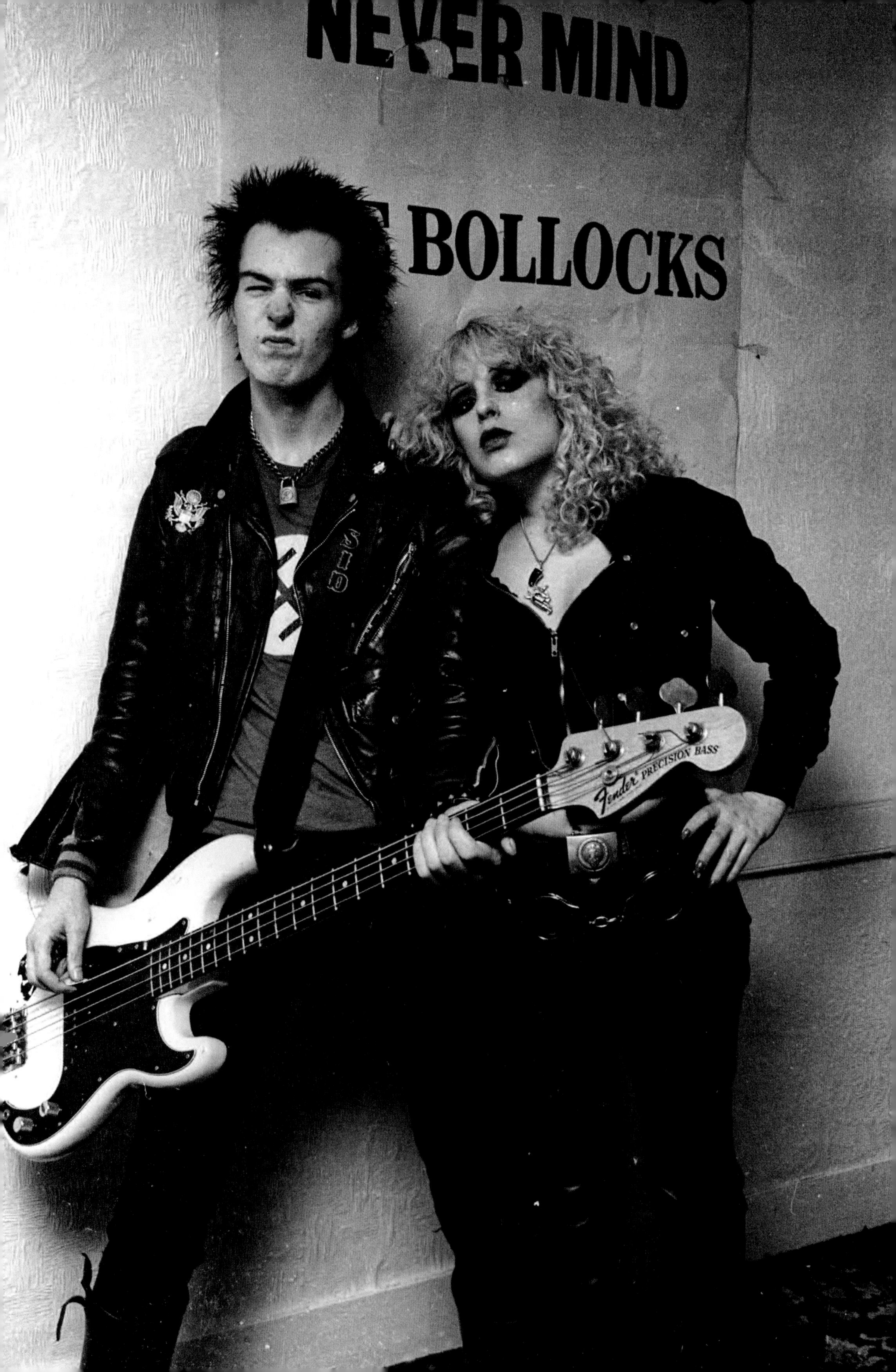

**THURSDAY**

**01**

**MARCH**

Scotland and Wales vote on devolution but both countries reject it. The referenda required the support of 40% of the electorate, not simply the majority of votes. This was not obtained in Scotland, although the majority of votes were in favour of devolution. Devolution was heavily defeated in Wales.

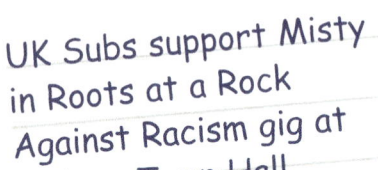

**FRIDAY**

**02**

**MARCH**

UK Subs support Misty in Roots at a Rock Against Racism gig at Fulham Town Hall, London.

**SATURDAY**

**10**

**MARCH**

Under the pseudonym The School Bullies, The Damned play at the Railway Hotel, West Hampstead, London.

**WEDNESDAY**
**28**
MARCH

As a result of the recent referenda, the Scottish Nationalists joined the Conservatives and Liberals in passing a vote of no confidence in James Callaghan's government, forcing a General Election.

**THURSDAY**
**29**
MARCH

James Callaghan announces that the General Election will be held on 3 May. All of the major opinion polls point towards a Conservative win which would make Margaret Thatcher the first female Prime Minister of Britain..

**FRIDAY**
**30**
MARCH

Airey Neave, World War Two veteran and Conservative Northern Ireland spokesman, is killed by an Irish National Liberation Army bomb in the House of Commons car park.

**WEDNESDAY**

**04**

**APRIL**

Josephine Whitaker, a 19-year-old bank worker, is murdered in Halifax; police believe that she is the 11th woman to be murdered by the Yorkshire Ripper.

**FRIDAY**

**13**

**APRIL**

Members debut album *At The Chelsea Nightclub* is released on Virgin.

The Radio Times notes of this weeks's BBC Radio 1's Roundtable: Debbie Harry joins Kid Jensen to review the week's new records. Ultra blonde, ultra bombshell Debbie Harry is turning her thoughts to the big screen. She is thinking of starring with Robert Fripp (who used to be in King Crimson) in a remake of Alphaville, a 1966 film by Jean-Luc Godard. Blondie are recording their fourth album, tentatively called Eat the Beat.

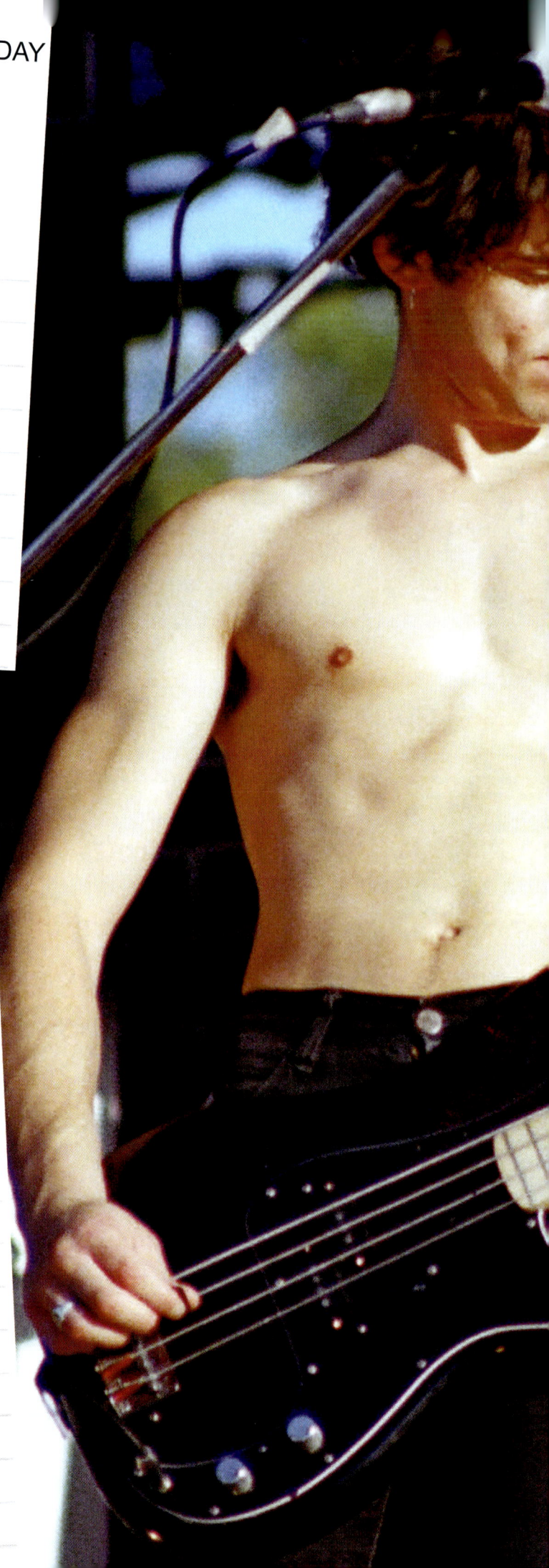

**SUNDAY 15 APRIL**

Stranglers' bass player JJ Burnel starts a solo tour in Glasgow promoting his *Euroman Cometh* album.

---

**THE STRANGLERS' EUROMAN COMETH**

Harvey Goldsmith Entertainments by arrangement with Black & White Management presents

# Jean Jacques Burnel
+ rapid eye movement
+ blood donor

SUN 15TH APRIL PAVILION GLASGOW
MON 16TH APRIL MANCHESTER APOLLO
TUE 17TH APRIL LIVERPOOL ERIC'S
WED 18TH APRIL DERBY ASSEMBLY ROOMS
FRI 20TH APRIL BIRMINGHAM, DIGBETH CIVIC HALL
SUN 22ND APRIL BRISTOL LOCARNO
TUE 24TH APRIL PORTSMOUTH LOCARNO
WED 25TH APRIL HEMEL HEMPSTEAD PAVILION
THU 26TH APRIL NEWCASTLE MAYFAIR
FRI 27TH APRIL EDINBURGH ODEON
SAT 28TH APRIL BRADFORD ST GEORGES HALL
SUN 29TH APRIL ILFORD ODEON

All Tickets £2.00 in advance £2.50 on door

**FRIDAY 20 APRIL**

Damned release 'Love Song'.

**MONDAY 23 APRIL**

Anti-Nazi League protestor Blair Peach is fatally injured after being struck on the head probably by a member of the Metropolitan Police's Special Patrol Group.

**FRIDAY 04 MAY**

The Conservatives win the General Election by a 43-seat majority and Margaret Thatcher becomes the first female Prime Minister of the United Kingdom. Liberal Party leader Jeremy Thorpe is the most notable MP to lose his seat in the election. Despite being 67 years old and having lost the first General Election he has contested, James Callaghan is expected to stay on as leader of a Labour Party now in opposition after five years in government.

**TUESDAY 08 MAY**

Former Liberal Party leader and MP Jeremy Thorpe goes on trial at the Old Bailey charged with attempted murder.

**SATURDAY 26 MAY**

Cameron Wildlife Park, Balloch is the venue for the first Loch Lomond Rock Festival. A two day event which includes on the Saturday, The Stranglers, Dr Feelgood. Third World, The Skids ,UK Subs and The Dickies. The Boomtown Rats and Buzzcocks are amongst the Sunday bands.

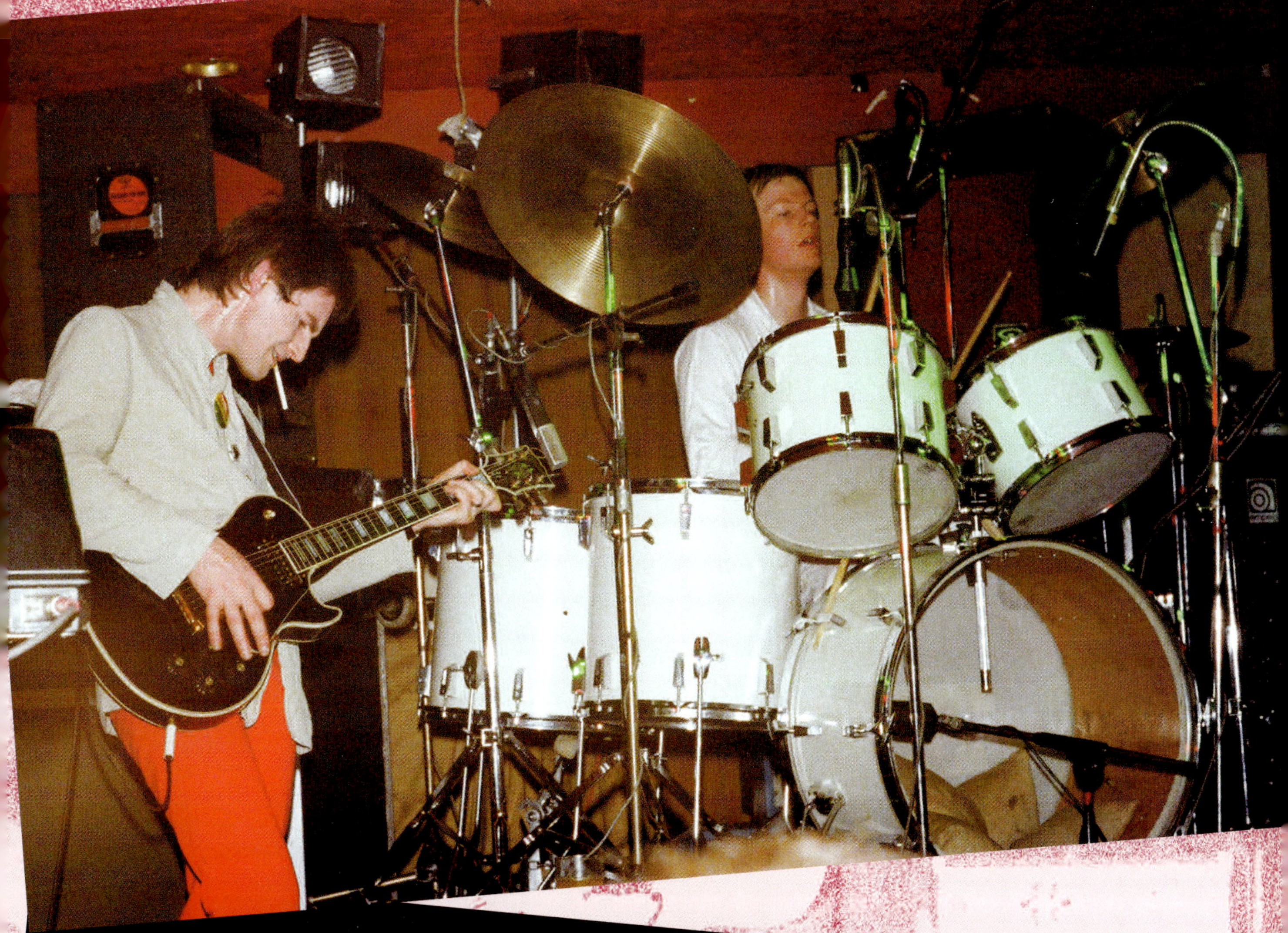

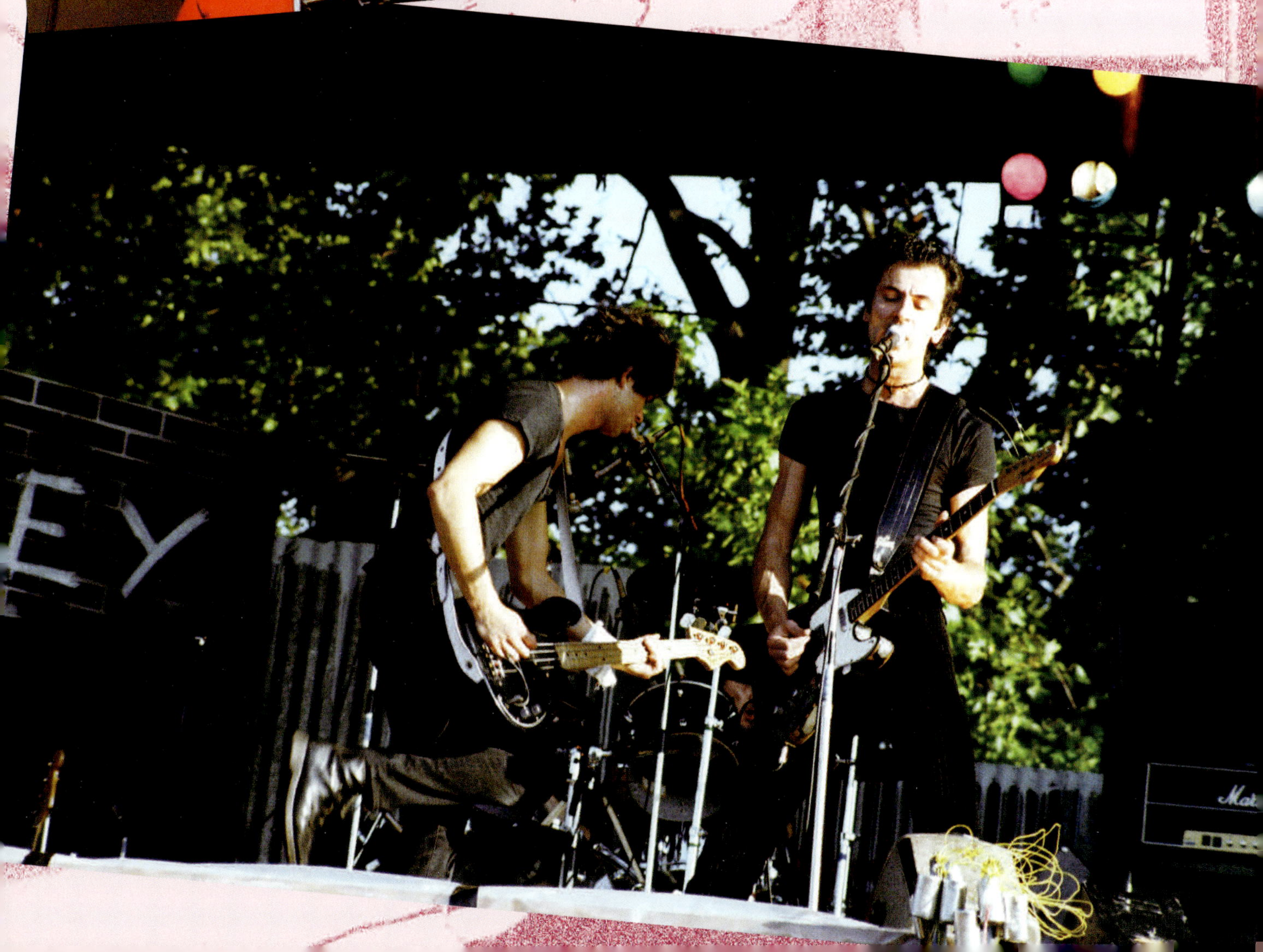

**THURSDAY**

**07**

Britain goes to the polls in the first direct election to the European Parliament. The turnout is 32%.

JUNE

**FRIDAY**

**15**

Generation X releases a special red vinyl edition single, 'Fridays Angels'. The standard black vinyl appears the following week.

JUNE

**FRIDAY**

**29**

Chelsea release their debut, self-titled album.

JUNE

**TUESDAY**

**17**

Athlete Sebastian Coe sets a record time for running a mile, completing it in 3 minutes 48.95 seconds.

JULY

**FRIDAY**

**27**

Angelic Upstarts release the single 'Teenage Warning'.

JULY

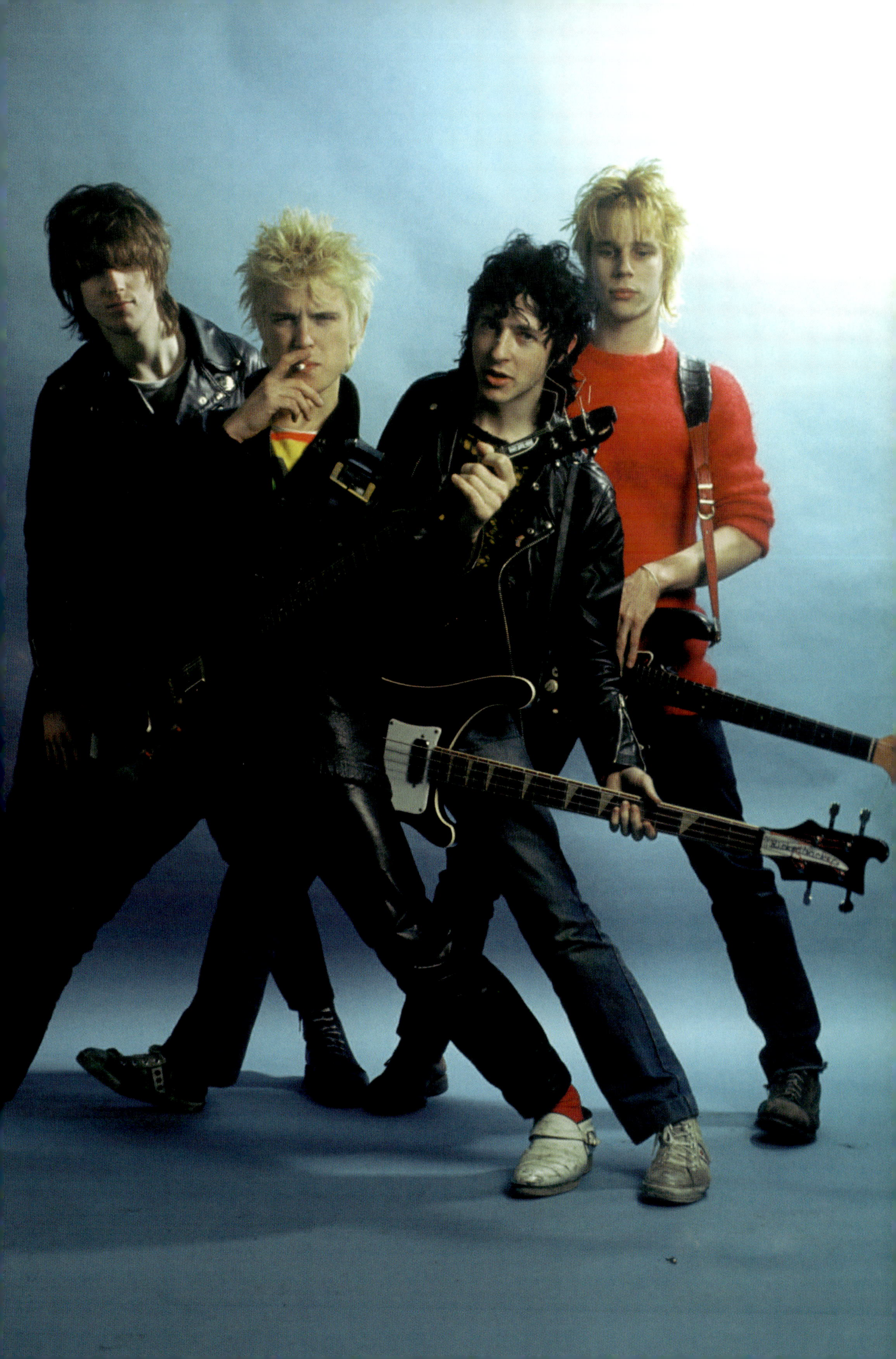

**THURSDAY**

**09**

A nudist beach is established in Brighton.

AUGUST

German singer Nina Hagen makes an infamous appearance on an Austrian evening talk show called *Club 2* in which she talks about and simulates masturbation.

*Rock 'n' Roll High School* film is released. It features music by The Ramones.

**FRIDAY**

**24**

AUGUST

**MONDAY**

**27**

AUGUST

Elizabeth II's cousin, Lord Louis Mountbatten, one of his teenage grandsons and two others were killed by a bomb planted on his boat at Mullaghmore in county Sligo, Ireland by the IRA. On the same day the IRA also killed 18 soldiers at Warrenpoint in County Down.

Also this month: Angelic Upstarts release their debut album, *Teenage Warning*.

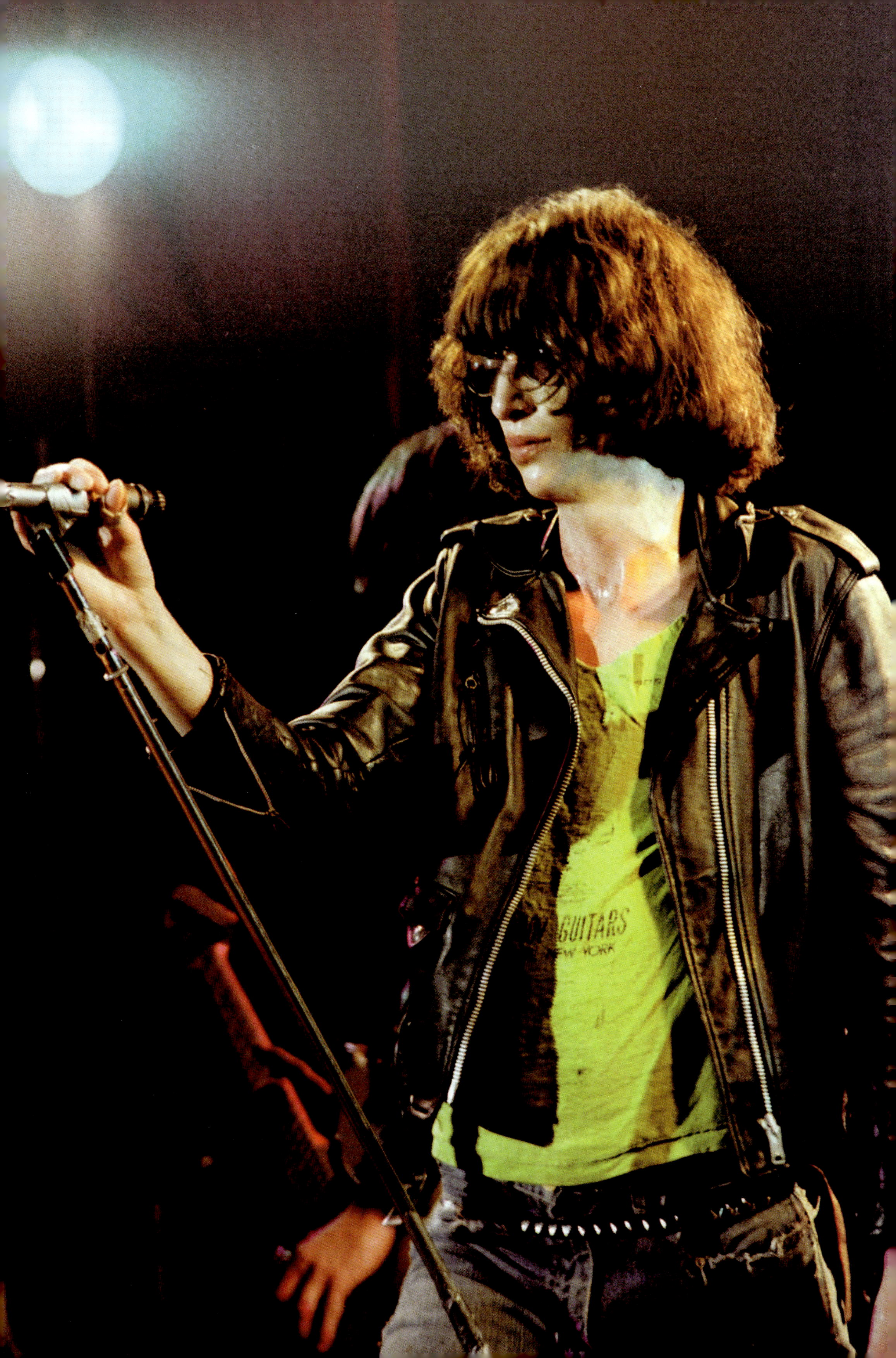
GUITARS

**SUNDAY**

**02**

Brixton Rock Against Racism carnival is cut short when Skinheads invade the stage during Stiff Little Fingers' set.

SEPTEMBER

Police discover a woman's body in an alleyway near Bradford city centre. The woman, 20-year-old student Barbara Leach, is believed to be the 12th victim of the mysterious Yorkshire Ripper mass murderer.

UK Subs first album, *Another Kind of Blues* is released.

**FRIDAY**

**14**

SEPTEMBER

Other albums released this month include:
The Slits debut, *Cut*.
Buzzcocks - *A Different Kind Of Tension*
Sham 69 - *Hersham Boys*
The Stranglers - *The Raven*

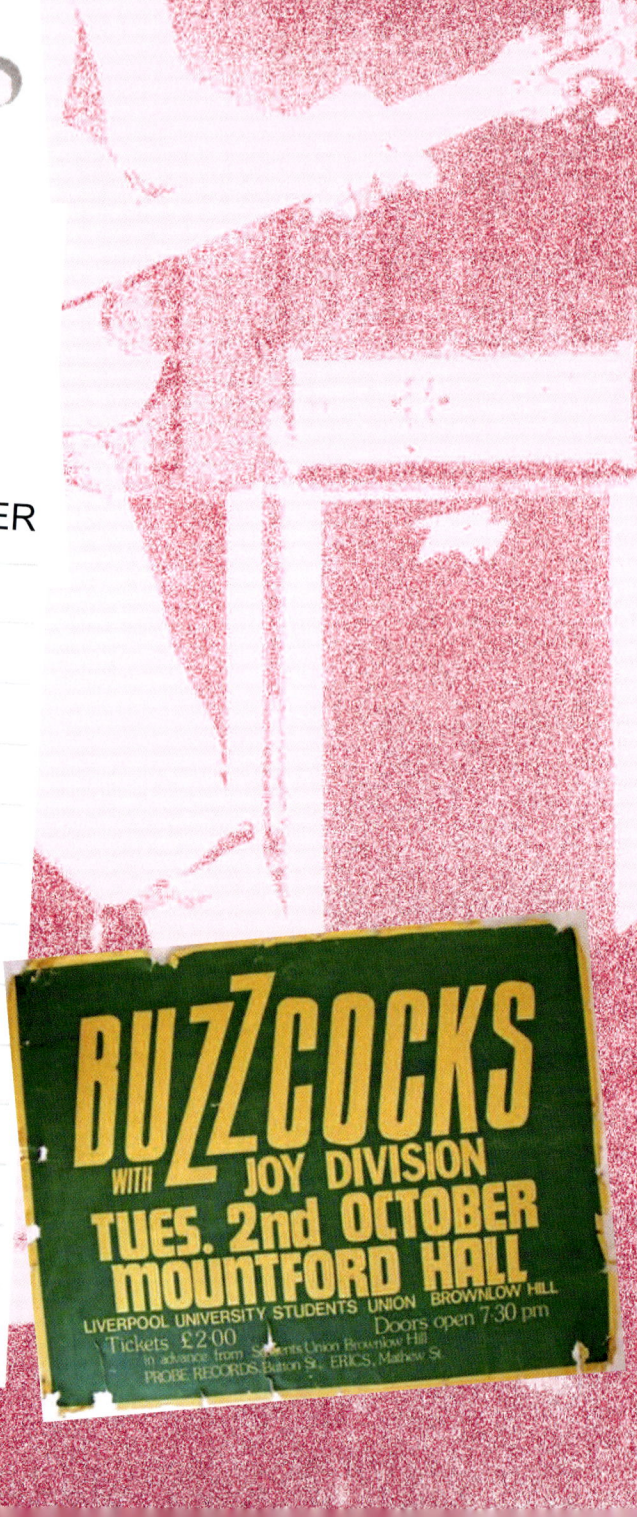

**BUZZCOCKS**
WITH JOY DIVISION
TUES. 2nd OCTOBER
MOUNTFORD HALL
LIVERPOOL UNIVERSITY STUDENTS UNION BROWNLOW HILL
Tickets £2.00 Doors open 7:30 pm
in advance from Students Union Brownlow Hill
PROBE RECORDS, Button St., ERICS, Mathew St.

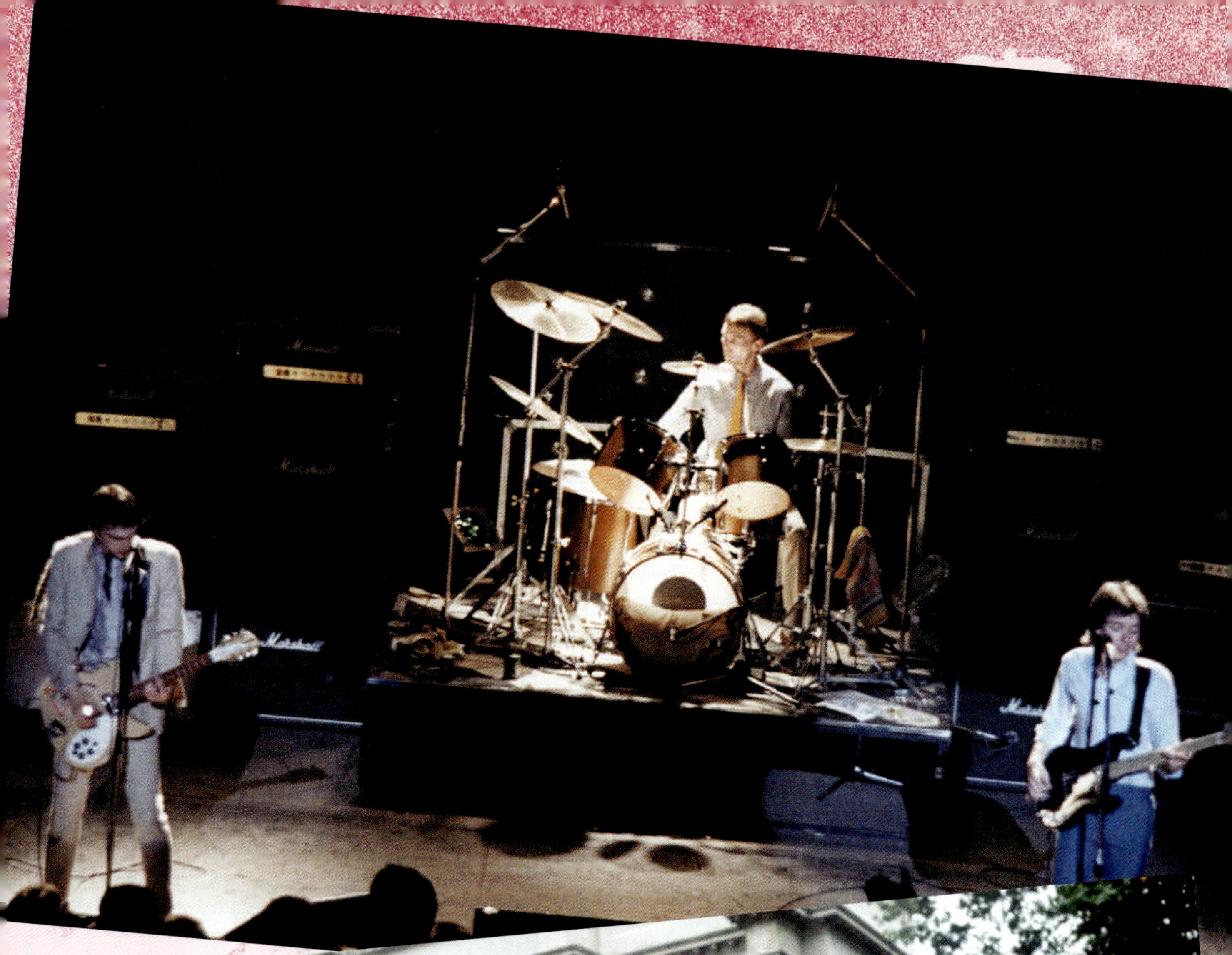
Marshall

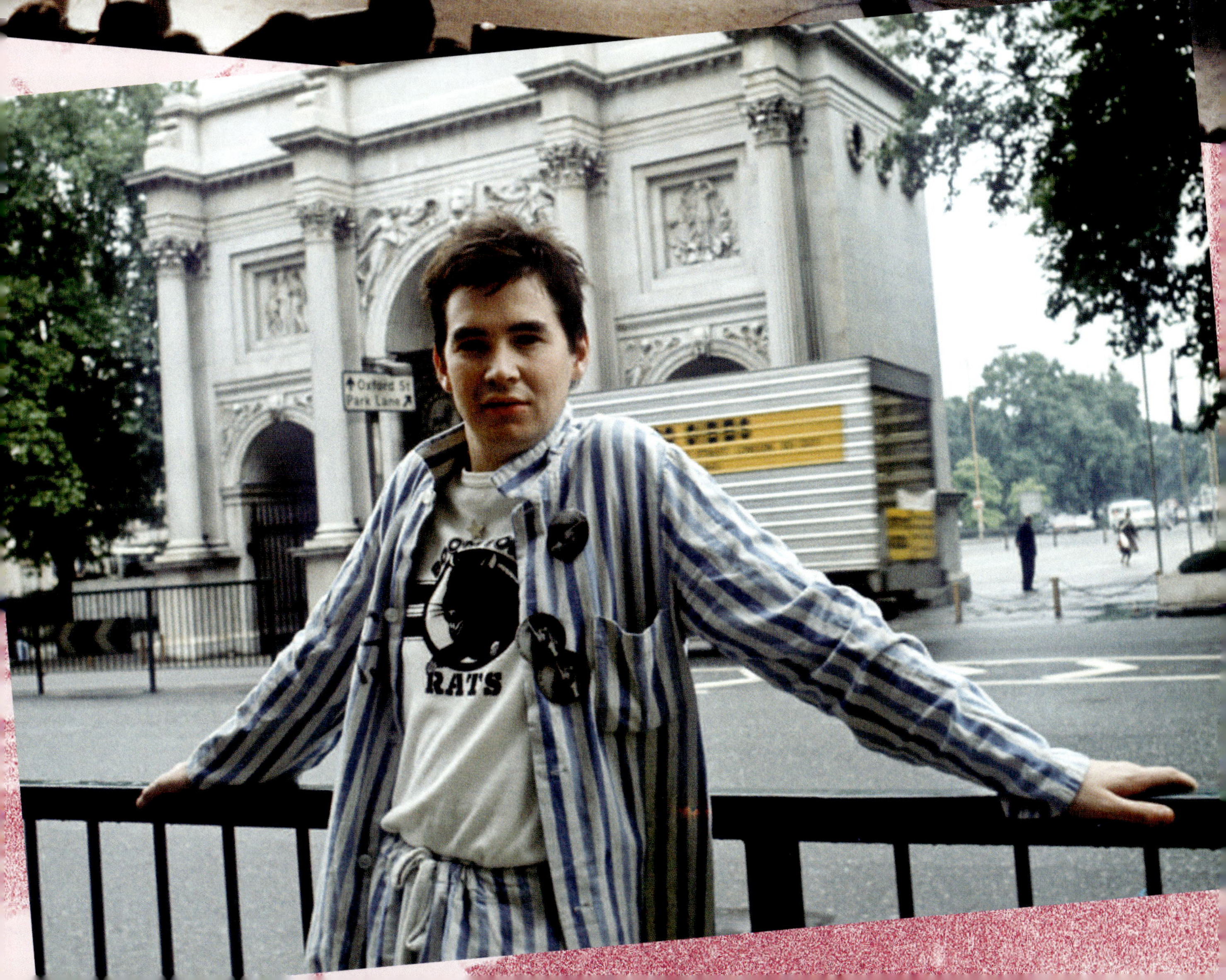
Oxford St
Park Lane
RATS

**THURSDAY**

**25**

OCTOBER

Final episode of the comedy series *Fawlty Towers* is broadcast on BBC2.

**SATURDAY**

**25**

OCTOBER

The Adverts play their last gig at Slough College.

**MONDAY**

**29**

OCTOBER

ITV debuts its comedy drama series *Minder* starring George Cole and Dennis Waterman.

**TUESDAY**

**30**

OCTOBER

Martin Webster of the National Front is found guilty of inciting racial hatred.

Virgin releases a Sex Pistols compilation album, *Flogging A Dead Horse* and the Adverts release *Cast Of Thousands*.

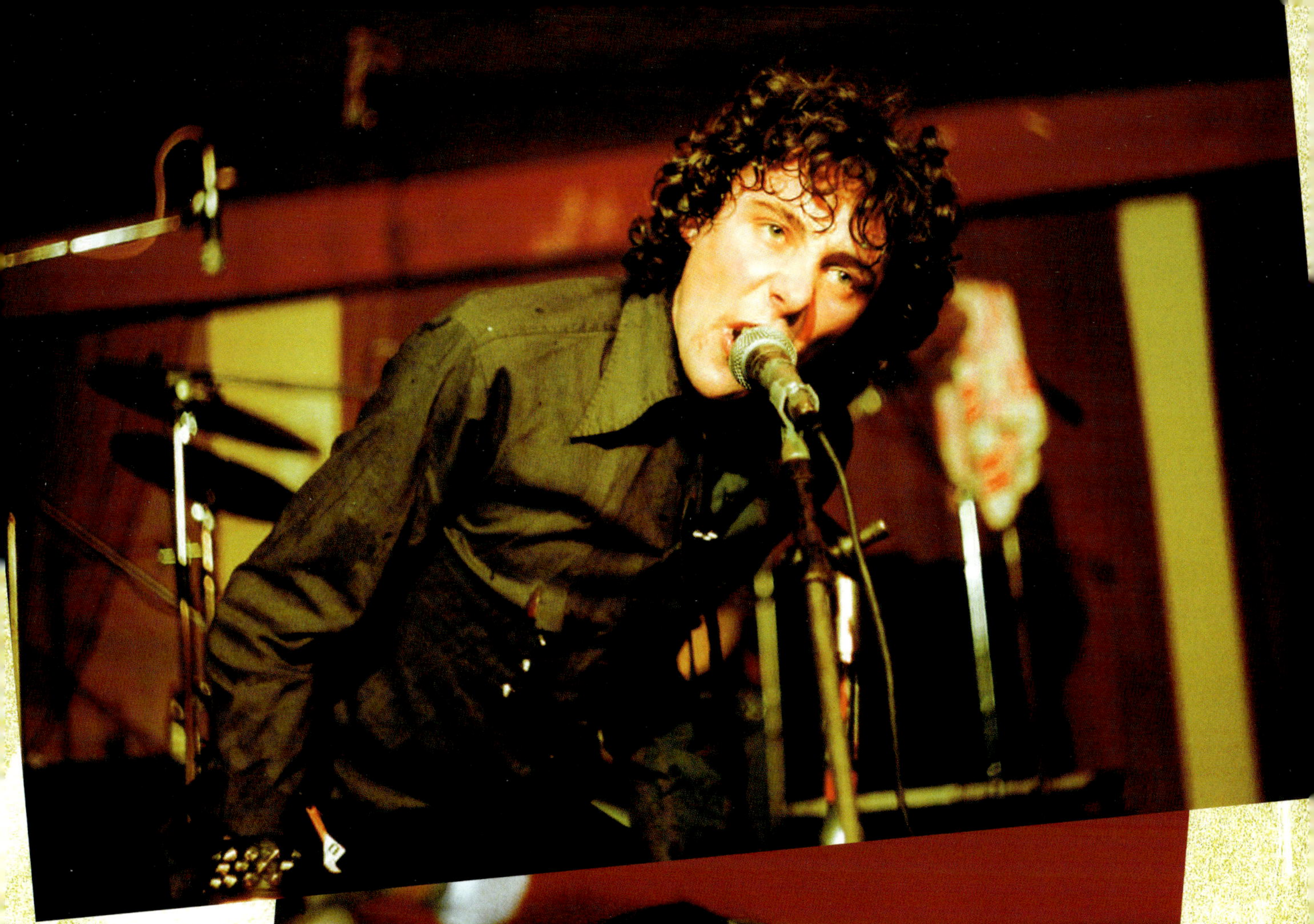

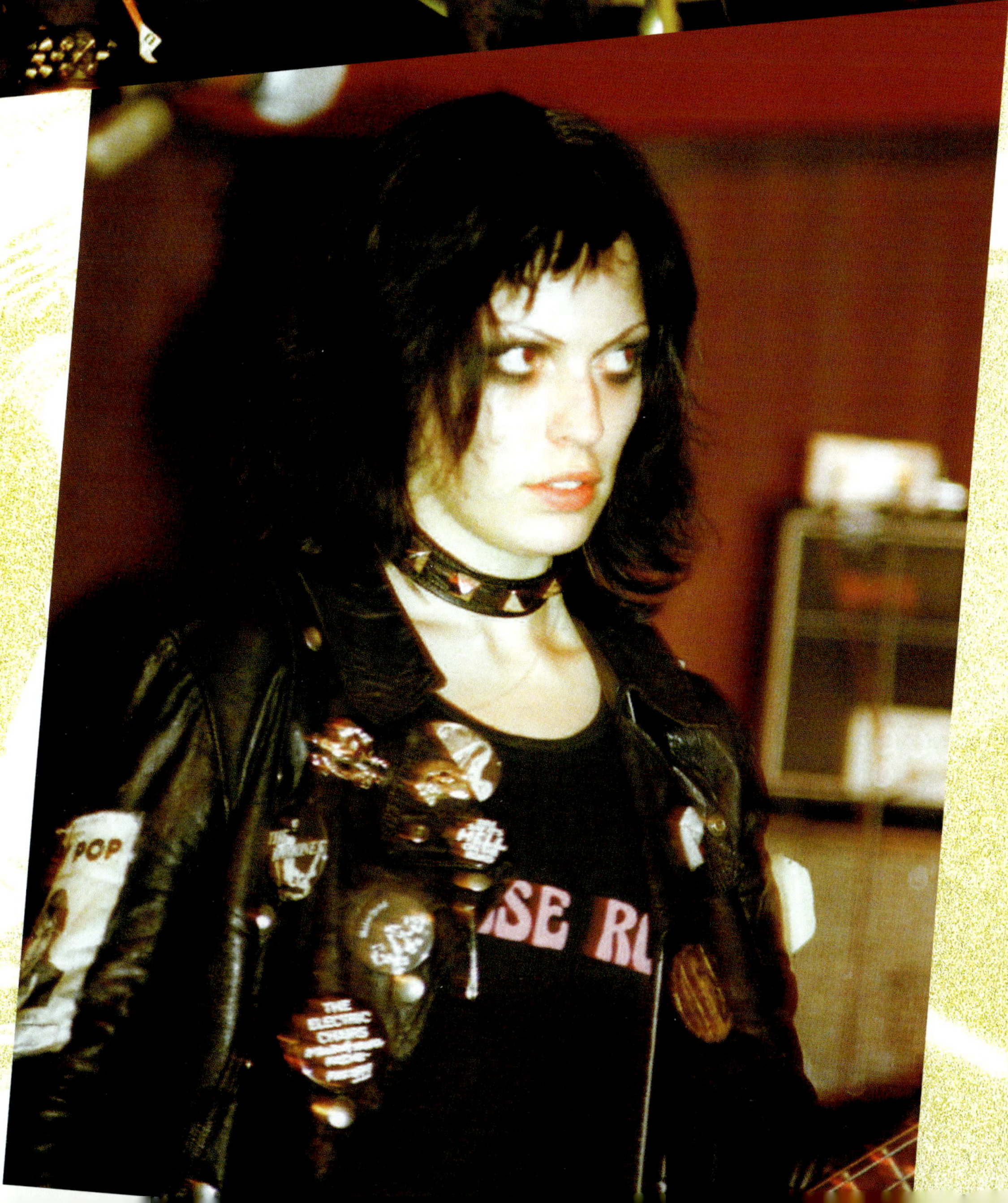
POP

**FRIDAY**

**23**

NOVEMBER

In Dublin, Ireland, Irish Republican Army member Thomas McMahon is sentenced to life in prison for the assassination of Lord Mountbatten.

Public Image Ltd release a triple LP in a round metal canister. It's called Metal Box.

**FRIDAY**

**14**

DECEMBER

The Clash release London Calling. The cover is a photo of Paul Simonon smashing his guitar against the stage at The Palladium in New York City on 20th September. The lettering used on the cover pays homage to Elvis Presely's debut album from 1956.

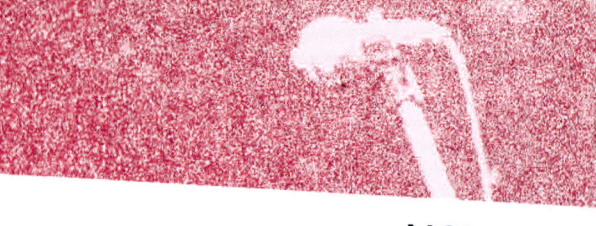

**MONDAY**

**10**

DECEMBER

The Stranglers start their second Japanese tour of the year.

**FRIDAY**

**28**

DECEMBER

The Stranglers cancel a tour of India because of "possible trouble" during elections there.

Also this month: Stations Of The Crass album by The Crass is released.

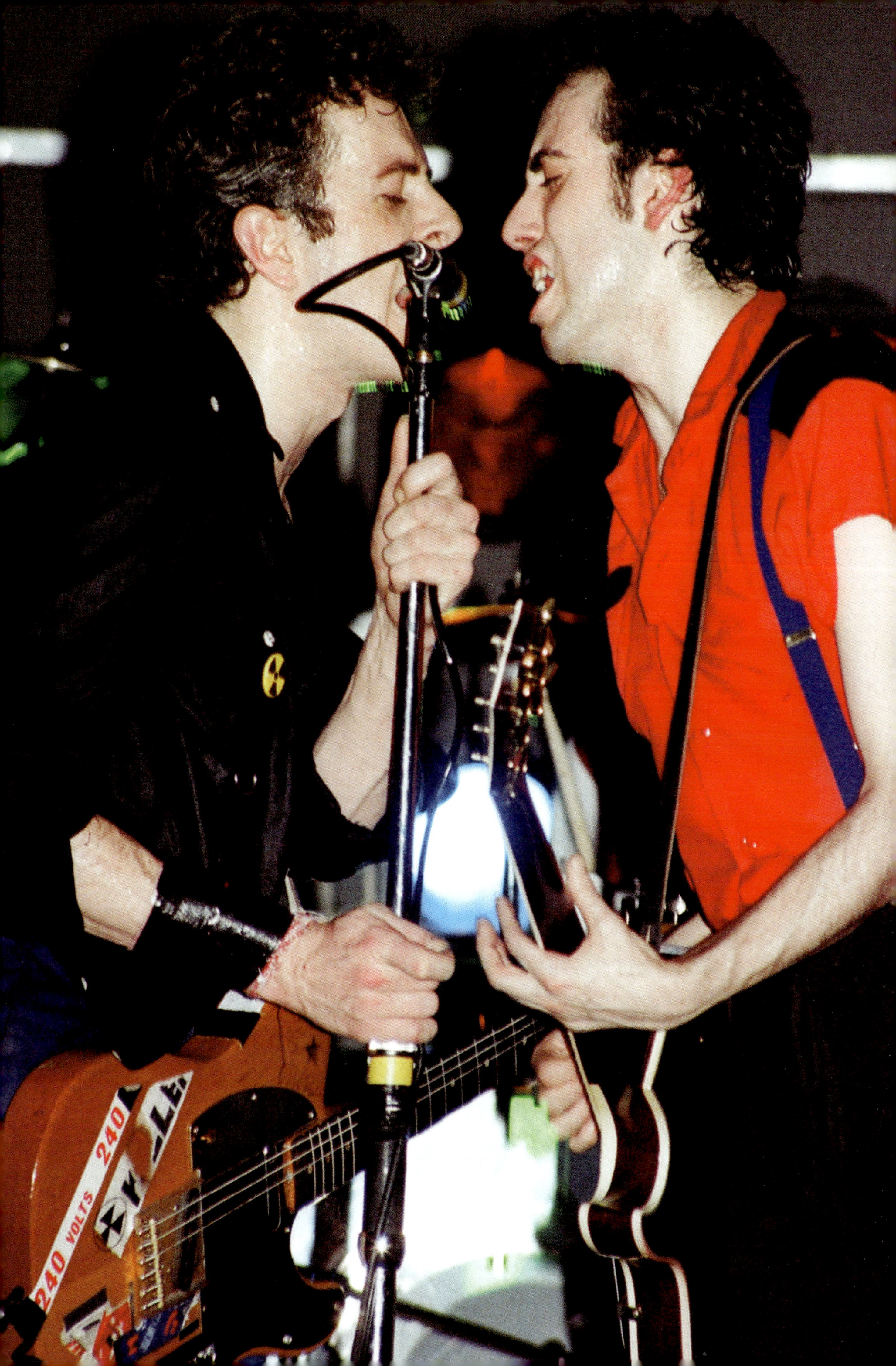
240
240 VOLTS

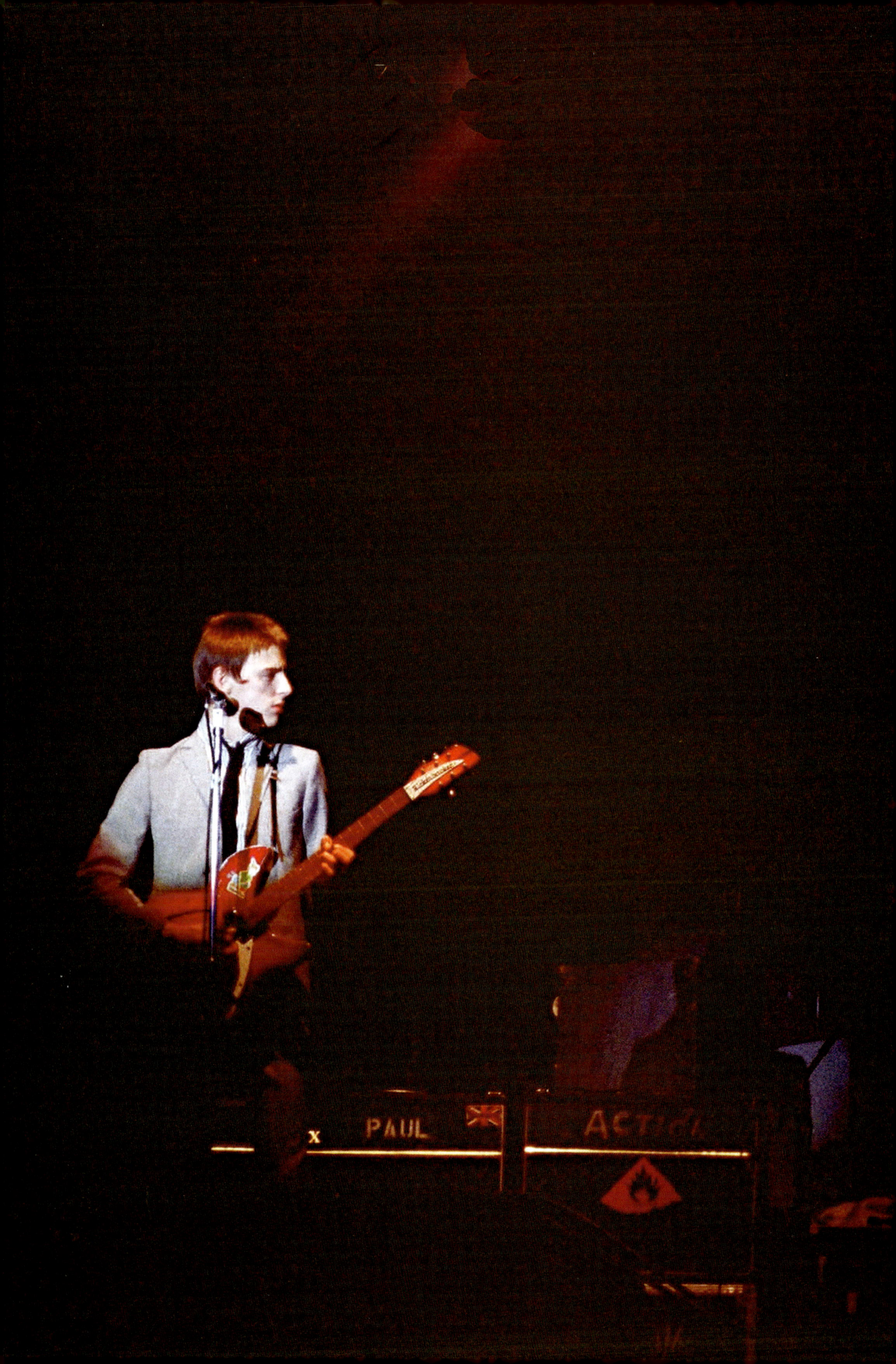
PAUL

# 1980

**WEDNESDAY**

**02**

JANUARY

Workers at British Steel Corporation go on a nationwide strike over pay called by the Iron and Steel Trades Confederation, which has some 90,000 members among British Steel's 150,000 workforce, in a bid to get a 20% rise. It is the first steelworks strike since 1926.

**MONDAY**

**07**

JANUARY

Hugh Cornwell gets a £300 fine and is sentenced to two months in gaol for drug possession.

**WEDNESDAY**

**13**

FEBRUARY

The Police break down the door of John Lydon's London house in a raid looking for illegal weapons. Lydon faces them waving a sword.

**FRIDAY**

**22**

FEBRUARY

Malcolm McLaren fires Adam Ant from the original Adam & The Ants and keeps the nucleus of the group to form Bow Wow.

Public Image Ltd release *Second Edition* LP.

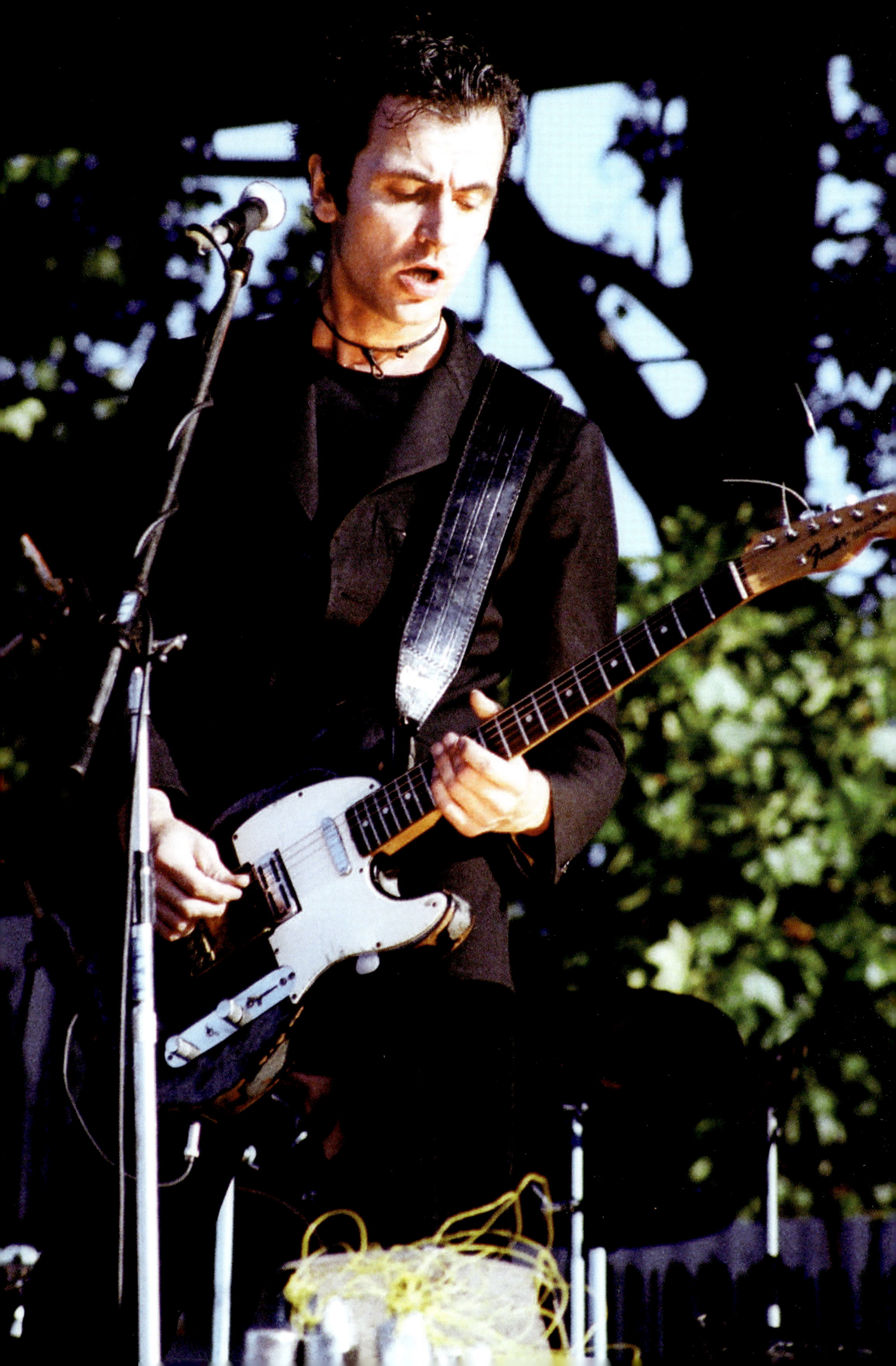
Fender

**FRIDAY**

**07**

MARCH

Cockney Rejects release their album *Greatest Hits Volume 1*.

**FRIDAY**

**21**

MARCH

High Cornwell loses his appeal against a two-month sentence for drug offences and goes straight to Pentonville Prison.

**SATURDAY**

**22**

MARCH

Barely a week after release, The Jam's 'Going Underground' hits number one.

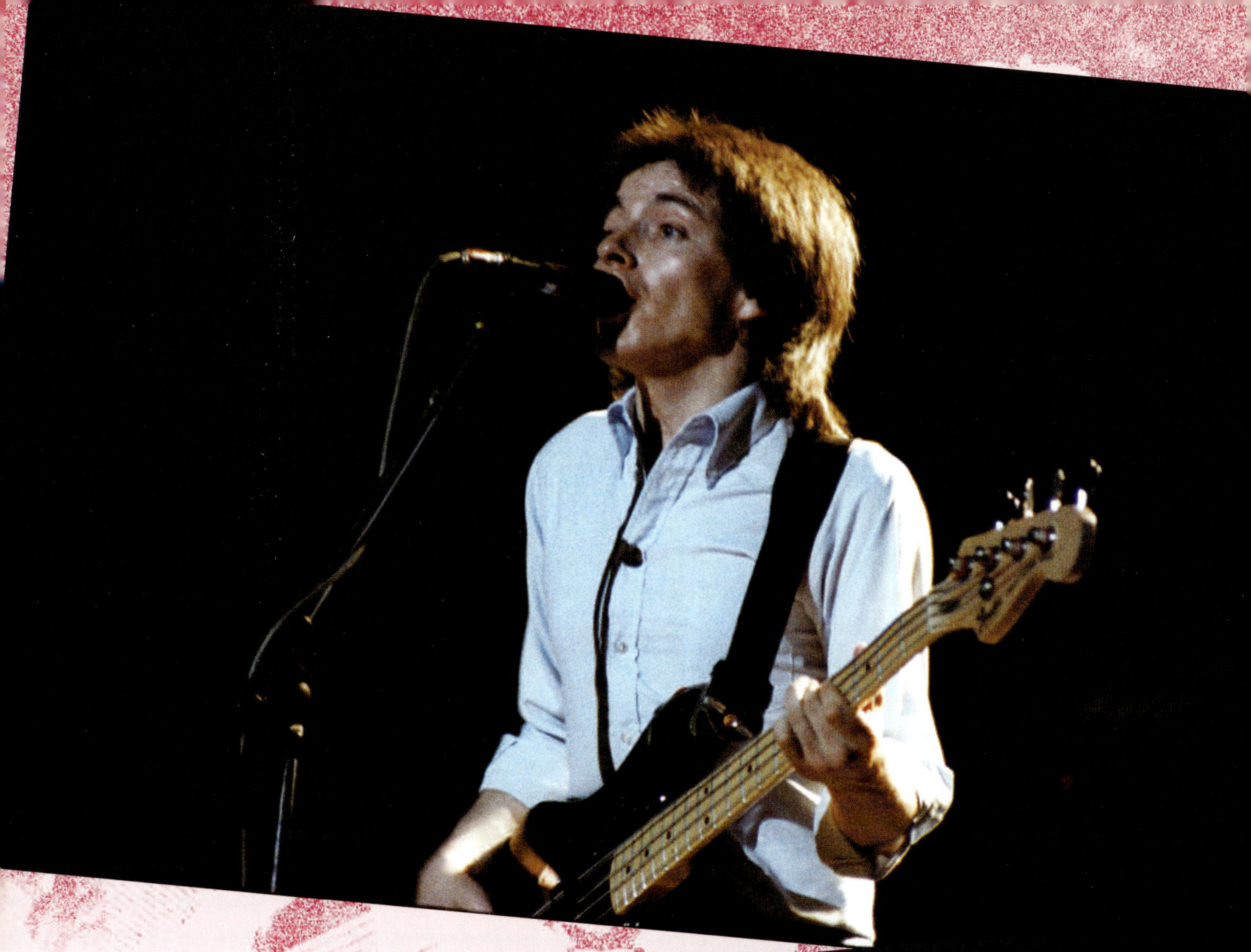

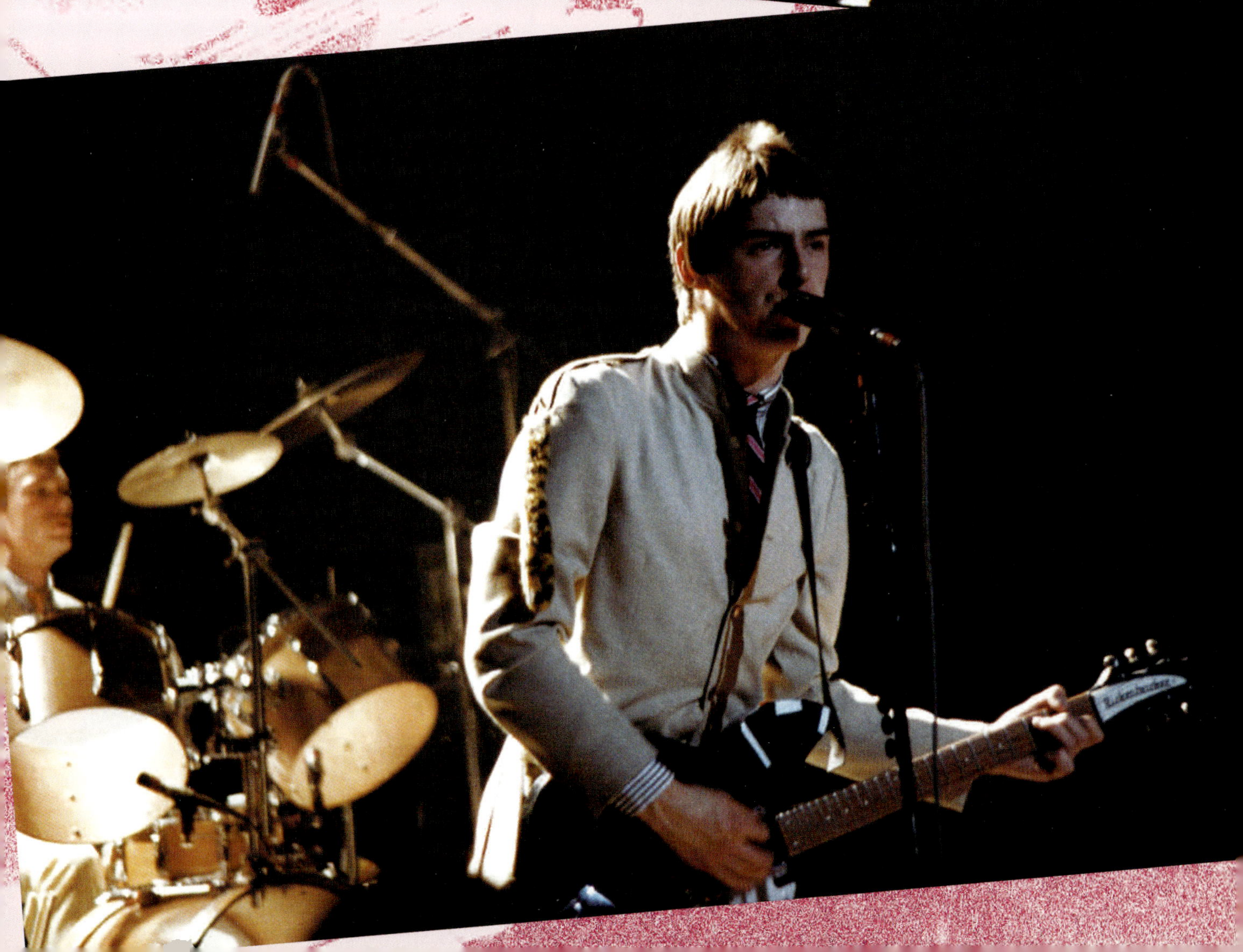

**FRIDAY**
**04**
APRIL

Sham 69 release 'Tell The Children'.

**TUESDAY**
**22**
APRIL

UK unemployment stands at a two-year high of more than 1.5million.

**WEDNESDAY**
**30**
APRIL

A six-man terrorist team calling itself the "Democratic Revolutionary Movement for the Liberation of Arabistan" (DRMLA) captures the Embassy of Iran in Prince's Gate, Knightsbridge, London.

Also this month:
Iggy Pop is banned from some UK venues because his backing band includes former Sex Pistol Glenn Matlock!

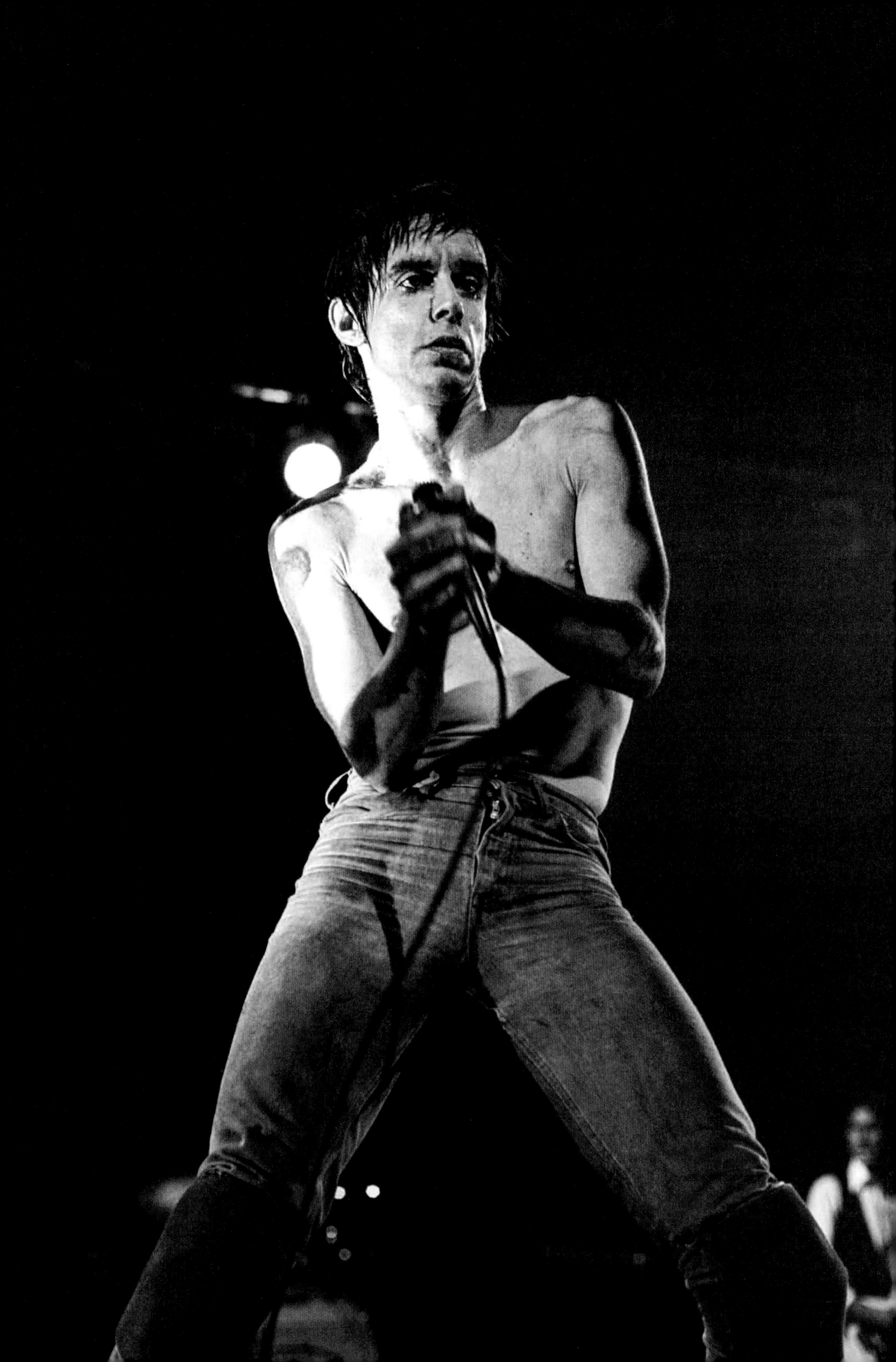

**FRIDAY**
**02**
MAY

Cockney Rejects release 'I'm Forever Blowing Bubbles' to celebrate West Ham reaching the F.A. Cup Final.

**MONDAY**
**05**
MAY

The SAS storm the Iranian Embassy building, killing 5 of the 6 terrorists and freeing all the hostages.

**TUESDAY**
**11**
MAY

Industrial action at EMI's factory holds up supplies of records to the shops.

**TUESDAY**

**15**

MAY

London opening of *The Great Rock 'n' Roll Swindle* film.

**SUNDAY**

**18**

MAY

Ian Curtis commits suicide.

**TUESDAY**

**20**

MAY

The Clash row with CBS over the release of 'Bank Robber' as a single: The record company think it's "uncommercial".

**SATURDAY**

# 21

**JUNE**

The Stranglers are arrested in Nice accused of starting a riot after walking off stage following a serious of power failures.

| TUESDAY | UK unemployment is announced to have reached a postwar high of 1,600,000. |
|---|---|
| **24** | |
| JUNE | |

| The Sony Walkman goes on sale in the United States. | WEDNESDAY |
|---|---|
| | **25** |
| | JUNE |

**TUESDAY**

**08**

JULY

Dead Kennedy's Jello Biafra runs for Mayor of San Fransisco. He doesn't succeed.

Miners threatening to strike demand a 37% pay increase, ignoring pleas from Margaret Thatcher to hold down wage claims.

**FRIDAY**

**18**

JULY

Funeral of Malcolm Owen of The Ruts.

Also this month:
Polydor releases a Punk compilation called, 20 Of Another Kind including tracks by Plastic Bertrand, The Jam, Skids, Otway And Barrett, Sham 69, The Cure, Stiff Little Fingers, The Adverts, Generation X, 999, The Stranglers, The Boys, Patrik Fitzgerald, The Jolt, The Heartbreakers and The Lurkers.

105

**FRIDAY**
# 15
**AUGUST**

A patron ejected from a Soho club returns with a can of petrol, lit a match and kills 37 people attending a farewell party - London's deadliest fire since the Blitz.

**FRIDAY**
Mecca Ballrooms ban the Dead Kennedys from their venues.
# 30
**AUGUST**

**YOUR WORST FEARS CONFIRMED**

**FRIDAY**
# 05
SEPTEMBER

Dead Kennedys release the *Fresh Fruit for Rotting Vegetables* LP

**SUNDAY**
# 21
SEPTEMBER

Dundee Council cancel the Dead Kennedys' gig at the Caird Hall.

**MONDAY**

**06**

OCTOBER

John Lydon sentenced to three months in gaol for assaulting Dublin barman Eamonn Brady and calling him an "Irish pig".

**TUESDAY**

**07**

OCTOBER

Having spent the weekend in custody the 23-year-old former Sex Pistols singer was freed on £750 bail while he waits for an appeal to be heard.

**WEDNESDAY**

**08**

OCTOBER

Dead Kennedys first London gig at the Music Machine stops when the stage is shared with at least 20 whirling invaders and two microphone are ripped from their sockets.

Also this month:
Police find a handgun and "certain substances" on Joe Strummer outside London's King's Cross Railway Station.

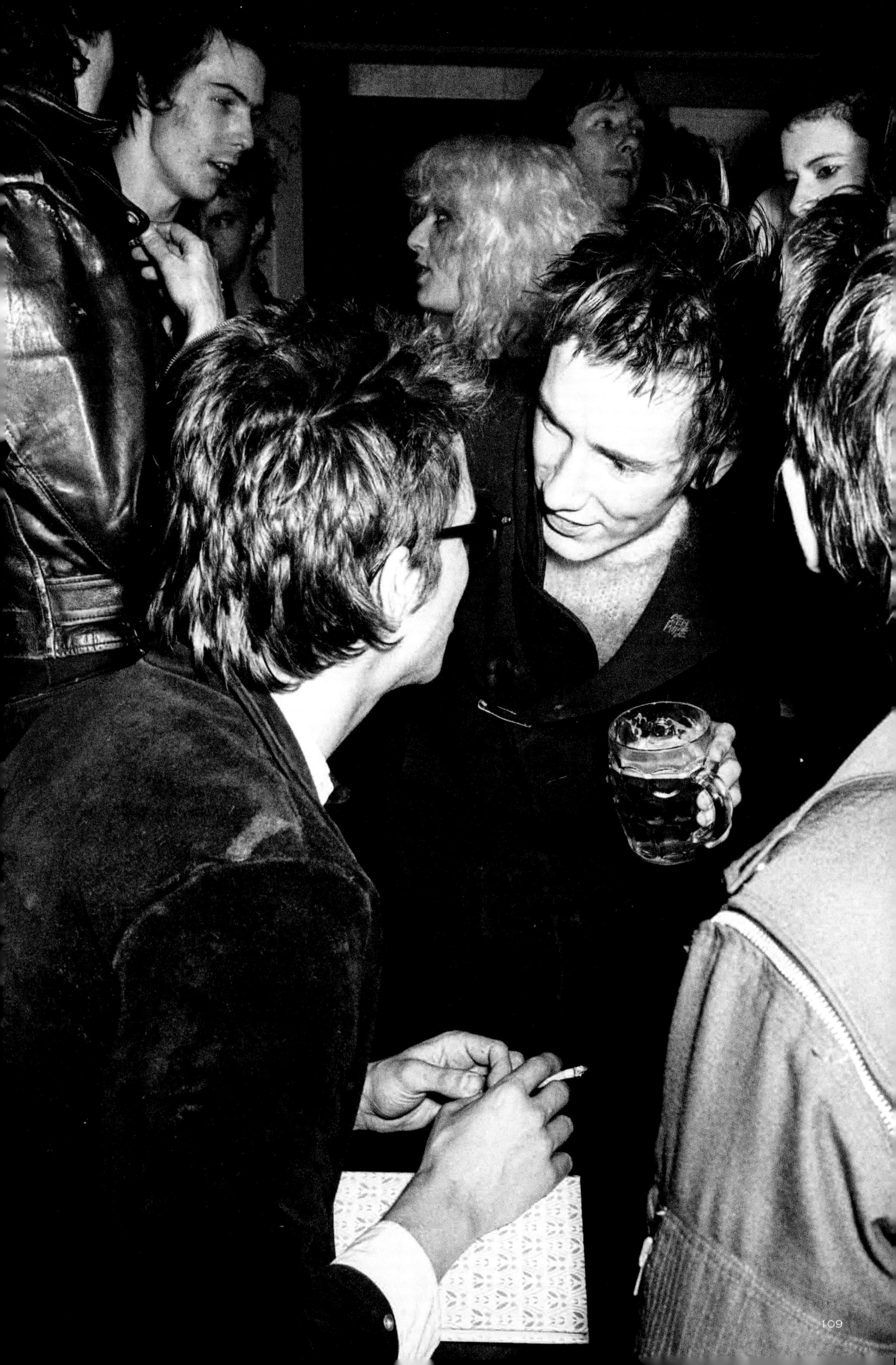

**MONDAY 17 NOVEMBER**

University student Jacqueline Hill, aged 20, is murdered in Headingley, Leeds.

**WEDNESDAY 19 NOVEMBER**

Police investigating the murder of Jacqueline Hill establish that she was probably the 13th woman to be killed by the Yorkshire Ripper.

---

**STRAIGHT MUSIC PRESENTS**

**KILLING JOKE**
**discharge**
**FAD GADGET**

LYCEUM
STRAND, W.C.2

SUNDAY 30th NOVEMBER at 7·30

TICKETS £3·00 (INC. VAT) ADVANCE LYCEUM BOX OFFICE, TEL. 836 3715, PREMIER BOX OFFICE, TEL: 240 2245, LONDON THEATRE BOOKINGS, SHAFTESBURY AVE., TEL: 439 3371, OR ROCK ON RECORDS, 3 KENTISH TOWN RD., NW1, TEL: 485 5088

---

**HAMMERSMITH ODEON**

**DEREK BLOCK presents**

**THE DAMNED**

**PLUS THE STRAPS**
**PLUS DAG VAG**

WEDNESDAY 3rd DECEMBER 7·30pm

TICKETS £3.50 £3·00 £2·50
AVAILABLE IN ADVANCE FROM BOX OFFICE 01-748 4081/2
PREMIER BOX OFFICE, LONDON THEATRE BOOKINGS and USUAL AGENTS

---

**MONDAY 08 DECEMBER**

John Lennon is shot dead by Mark Chapman after giving the murderer his autograph outside his apartment in New York.

---

**Public bard**

JOHN COOPER CLARKE, back from representing his country at the recent Poetry Olympics, has lined up a series of gigs before Christmas.

He appears at Sheffield Limit Club December 2, Edinburgh Playhouse 5, London The Venue 11, Liverpool Brady's 13, London Institute Of Contemporary Arts 15.

---

**X factor**

GENERATION X finally come out of hiding with a British club tour starting this weekend and an album in January.

They kick off at West Runton Pavilion on December 6 and then play Leeds Fan Club 7, Manchester Polytechnic 10, Middlesbrough Rock Garden 11, Retford Porterhouse 12, Sheffield Limit Club 18, Scarborough Taboo Club 19, Liverpool Brady's 20. A London gig is still being finalised.

---

Also this month: Billy Idol and Tony James reactivate Generation X with ex-Chelsea guitarist James Stevenson and former Clash drummer Terry Chimes. The new band is called Gen X.

---

**PUNK**

STRAIGHTS IN SHINY BLACK P.V.C., WITH ZIPS.

Men's 24" to 38" waist.
Girls' sizes 8 to 16.
ONLY £5.99 + £1.01 P&P

FAST DELIVERY
THE CHEAPEST AND THE BEST IN THE U.K.

Send cheques, PO's or cash to:
KANDA FASHIONS
(Dept S) Ltd
Bannerman Road, Easton,
Bristol BS5 0rr

---

**Buzz off**

THE BUZZCOCKS have cancelled the second part of their 'occasional tour', which was due to begin this weekend. It's because of recording commitments and the band have expressed their disappointment. They hope to reschedule some of the dates around Christmas. Tickets can be refunded at the point of purchase.

---

**Bow wowee**

BOW WOW WOW play the last of their Saturday residencies at the Hammersmith Starlight Roller Disco on December 6 and then head out for their first provincial dates.

The band, who've just released an eight-track cassette, which is not available in record form, play Leeds Warehouse December 8 (matinee and evening show), Nottingham Boat Club 9, Keele University 10, Scarborough Taboo 12, Edinburgh Nite Club (matinee and evening show) 13, Ayr Pavilion (matinee only) 14, Manchester Polytechnic 16, Cromer West Runton Pavilion 18, Birmingham Cedar Ballroom (matinee and evening show) 19, Sheffield Limit Club (matinee only) 20, Bristol Granary 22.

The support groups will be local bands. Another London gig is also being lined up for Christmas and details should be announced

---

**Stranglers face frog march to prison**

THE STRANGLERS got off to a grim start when they travelled down to Nice last week to defend themselves against charges of inciting a riot at Nice University during their much-publicised concert there in June.

The French prosecutor asked for a year's sentence for Jean Jacques Burnel for shouting at the crowd in French and six months for Jet Black and Hugh Cornwell because they only shouted in English. The judge will give his verdict next month.

# Undertones tear up contract with Sire

**THE UNDERTONES**, who set out on their 'See No More' tour next week, have split from Sire Records after a number of 'irreconcilable' differences.

The band signed to Sire in September 1978 and have released two albums and seven singles. These will continue to be available to the end of March, when the rights will revert back to the group.

Quite what the 'irreconcilable differences' are hasn't been revealed, but the fact that the band have been able to leave the label and take all their material with them suggests that the contract they originally signed might not have been held to be legally binding in a court.

They are now considering "various methods of releasing future records", which could mean they will not be signing a normal record company contract. They intend to release a new single in January and say that they will be spending more time touring next year now that their contractual hassles are over.

They were hoping to play some additional Irish dates before Christmas, but these have now been postponed and a two-week Irish tour is being lined up for February.

Sire Records has just been acquired by Warner brothers, who have taken a 100 per cent interest in the company. Founder Seymour Stein will continue as president and as far as Britain is concerned it will continue to operate as a separate company. The label will concentrate on signing and promoting acts while Warner Brothers will handle all the 'non-creative' functions, such as pressing and distribution.

# Rats pack

**THE BOOMTOWN RATS** have announced details of their British tour, which starts early in January and forms the first leg of a world trip. It will follow the release of their fourth album, 'Mondo Bongo', which was delayed after a dispute between the band and Phonogram International.

The album will now be released on December 26 — a peculiar release date to say the least! It contains twelve tracks including a five-minute version of their single, 'Banana Republic', and a song called 'Under Their Thumb', with music by Jagger and Richards and words by the Rats.

The tour begins at Southampton Gaumont on January 4, followed by Bristol Colston Hall 5, Cardiff Sophia Gardens 6, Birmingham Odeon 7, Leicester De Montfort Hall 9, Manchester Apollo 10, Newcastle City Hall 11, Glasgow Apollo 13, Edinburgh Odeon 14, Sheffield City Hall 16, London Hammersmith Odeon 17.

Tickets are £3.50, £3.00 and £2.50 everywhere except Cardiff where they are all £3.50. They go on sale at the venues this Saturday.

# Hazel goes nuts

**HAZEL O'CONNOR**, who completes her British tour this week coinciding with the release of her second album 'Sons And Lovers' on Albion, has lined up another batch of dates for January.

She'll be taking in places not covered by the first tour and starts at York University 18, continuing at Glasgow Tiffany's on January 18, Oxford Polytechnic 23, Coventry 20, Bradford St George's Hall 21, Oxford Polytechnic 23, Coventry Theatre 24, Bath Pavilion 25, Exeter University 26, Worthing Assembly Rooms 29.

---

STRAIGHT MUSIC PRESENTS

## Ian Dury & The Blockheads

WITH GUESTS

**THE SELECTER** **BASEMENT 5** and **Blurt**

MICHAEL SOBELL CENTRE
HORNSEY RD, ISLINGTON N7

SUN/MON/TUE 21st/22nd/23rd DEC at 7-30

TICKETS £4.00 INC. VAT. ADVANCE M.S. CENTRE BOX OFFICE, TEL: 607 1632
LONDON THEATRE BOOKINGS, SHAFTESBURY AVE. TEL: 439 3371; PREMIER BOX OFFICE, TEL: 240 2245;
ROCK ON RECORDS, 3 KENTISH TOWN RD., NW1. TEL: 485 5088, OR £4.00 ON NIGHT

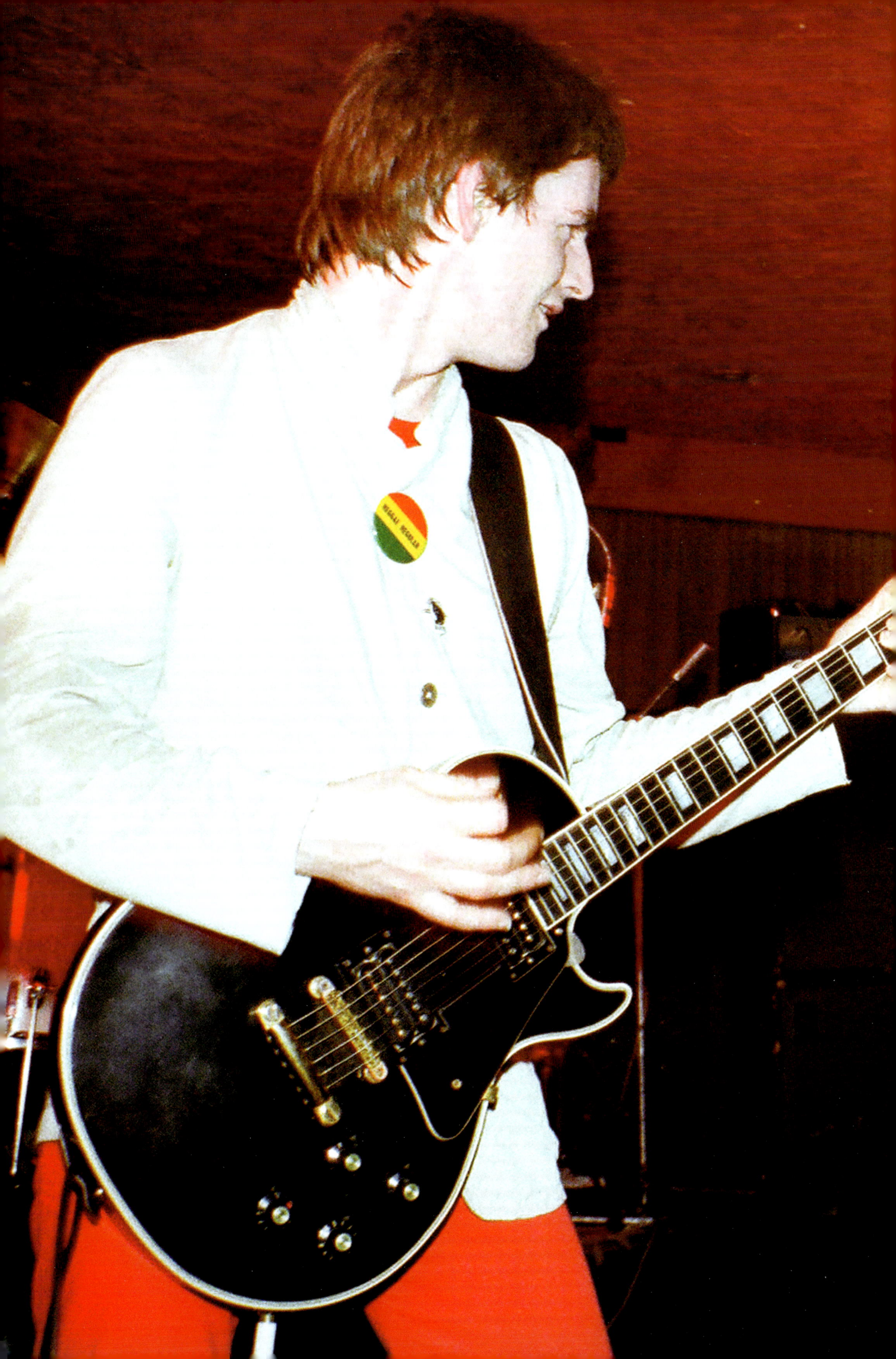

1981

MONDAY

## 05

JANUARY

Peter Sutcliffe, a 35-year-old lorry driver from Bradford arrested three days earlier in Sheffield, is charged with being the notorious serial killer known as the "Yorkshire Ripper", who is believed to have murdered 13 women and attacked seven others across northern England since 1975.

A parcel bomb addressed to the Prime Minister is intercepted at the sorting office.

WEDNESDAY

## 07

JANUARY

**Skins man**
THE 4-SKINS have now been joined by former Cockney Rejects drummer Nigel Wolfe. He makes his first appearance with the band at a punk convention at Southgate Alan Pullinger Centre on January 9.

SUNDAY

## 18

JANUARY

Eleven young black people are killed and thirty are injured in an arson attack on a house in New Cross, London.

Also this month:
The Stranglers are informed no further action will be taken following their arrests in Nice the previous year. Drummer Jet Black promises to publish his account of the event in a book to be called *Much Ado About Nothing*.

**FRIDAY 13 FEBRUARY**

The National Coal Board announces widespread pit closures.

**SATURDAY 14 FEBRUARY**

Gen X break up. Billy Idol leaves for the States to start a solo career.

The Jam play a secret gig at The Cricketers pub in their hometown of Woking. The NME reports, it ends in tears with fans unconscious and one group member, Bruce Foxton observed in an altercation with bar staff.

**FRIDAY 20 FEBRUARY**

Four MPs announce their intention to leave the Labour Party.

Peter Sutcliffe is charged with the murder of 13 women in the north of England.

---

**Derek Block in association with Dave Woods presents**

**Siouxsie and the Banshees**

PLUS COMSAT ANGELS

Feb 16/17   HAMMERSMITH PALAIS   7.30 pm
All tickets £3.50 available from the Palais 01-748 2812 and usual agents.

Feb 19   POOLE ARTS CENTRE   7.30 pm
(Wessex Hall)
Tickets £3.50, £3.00 in advance from Box Office. (Poole) 85222

Feb 20th   PORTSMOUTH GUILDHALL   7.30 pm
Tickets £3.50, £3.00 in advance from Box Office. 0705 24355

Feb 22nd   DE MONFORT HALL, LEICESTER   7.30 pm
Tickets £3.50, £3.00 in advance from Box Office. 0533 54444

Feb 23   ASSEMBLY ROOMS, DERBY   7.30 pm
Tickets £3.50, £3.00 in advance from Box Office. 0332 31111

Feb 25th   LEEDS UNIVERSITY S.U.   8 pm
All tickets £3.50. Available from Students Union. 0532 39071

Feb 27   EDINBURGH PLAYHOUSE   7.30 pm
Tickets £3.50, £3.00 in advance from Box Office. 031-557 2590

March 1   ROYAL COURT, LIVERPOOL   7.30 pm
Tickets £3.50, £3.00 in advance from Box Office. 051-708 7411

March 2   KING GEORGE'S HALL, BLACKBURN   7.30 pm
Tickets £3.50, £3.00 in advance from Box Office. 0254 58424 & usual agents.

March 3   NEWCASTLE CITY HALL   7.30 pm
Tickets £3.50, £3.00 in advance from Box Office. 0632 612606

---

**FRIARS** AT THE MAXWELL HALL AYLESBURY
FRIDAY FEBRUARY 13th 7.30 p.m.
**U.K. SUBS**
+ THE STIFFS
+ ANTI-PASTI

AC Sound & Vision
Tickets 2.75 from Earth Records, Aylesbury. Scorpion, High Wycombe. Old Town Records, Hemel Hempstead. F.L. Moore Bletchley Luton & Dunstable. D.J. Holland, Leighton Buzzard. HI-VU Buckingham. Music Market, Oxford or 2.75 at door if available. Life membership 25p. Min age 16. Teenage.

---

STRAIGHT MUSIC PRESENTS
**THE SPIZZLES** (Athletico Spizz '80)
**SUBWAY SECT**
**MARTIAN DANCE**   **U.K. DECAY**
LYCEUM STRAND, WC2
SUNDAY 22nd FEBRUARY at 6-30
TICKETS £3-00 (INC. VAT) ADVANCE LYCEUM BOX OFFICE, TEL. 836 3715
LONDON THEATRE BOOKINGS, SHAFTESBURY AVE., TEL. 439 1371
OR ROCK ON RECORDS

---

Fresh Record Night
**U.K. DECAY**
MANUFACTURED ROMANCE, BIG HAIR
at DINGWALLS on MONDAY FEB 16th
Admission £1.75

### SATURDAY
# 21
UK unemployment now stands at 2,400,000: 10% of the workforce.

### MARCH

Also this month:
Buzzcocks announce a split. Pete Shelley is to go solo and drummer John Maher is joining the Invisible Girls.
*Elgin Avenue Breakdown* is a compilation album released by The 101ers, Joe Strummer's band before he joined The Clash.

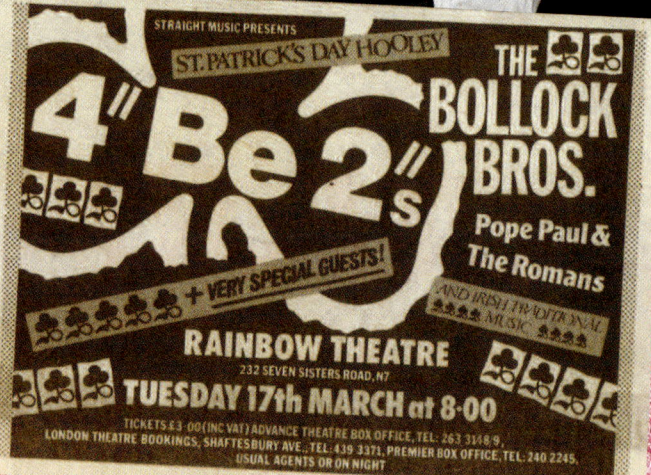

# COCKNEY REJECTS
## NEW E·P!
### Easy Life + Motorhead + Hang 'Em High

## Out of a Rut

RUTS DC step out for their first British tour, since Malcolm Owen's death last summer, at the end of this month. And they have a new album called 'Animal Now' set for release on May 8 by Virgin.

The band, who are now back up to a four-piece with the addition of Gary Barnacle on saxaphone, start their tour at Manchester Polytechnic April 30, Birmingham Cedar Club May 1, Liverpool Royal Court 2, Edinburgh Nite Club 6, Middlesbrough Rock Garden 7, Scarborough Penthouse 8, West Runton Pavilion 9, Brighton Jenkinsons 10, Cheltenham Technical College 12, London Lyceum 14.

More dates will be added to this schedule in the next week or so.

---

### The LYCEUM
**Outlaw Presents**
## THE RUTS D.C.
### CUBAN HEELS
### THE GAS
**THURSDAY 14th MAY 8pm**
ALL TICKETS £3·00
FROM BOX OFFICE, PREMIER BOX OFFICE, LONDON THEATRE BOOKINGS, & USUAL AGENTS
(SUBJECT TO BOOKING FEES)

**WEDNESDAY 01 APRIL**
NME's April fool joke that former Cream drummer Ginger Baker was joining Public Image Ltd gets widely reported in the National Press.

**FRIDAY 10 APRIL**
Public Image Ltd release *The Flowers of Romance* album.

**SATURDAY 11 APRIL**
Racial tensions following the arrest of a local black man spark riots in Brixton, South London.

**MONDAY 13 APRIL**
MP Enoch Powell warns that Britain "has seen nothing yet" with regards to racial unrest.

**FRIDAY 23 APRIL**
UK unemployment passes the 2,500,000 mark for the first time in nearly 50 years

**Nick nick**
CLASH drummer Nicky Headon was given a year's conditional discharge at London's Horseferry Road Magistrates Court last week when he admitted possessing quantities of cocaine and heroin.

**WEDNESDAY 13 APRIL**
Peter Sutcliffe admits to the manslaughter of 13 women on the grounds of diminished responsibility, but the judge rules that a jury should rule on Sutcliffe's state of mind before deciding whether to accept his plea or find him guilty of murder.

Also this month:
*Punks Not Dead* the debut studio album by The Exploited is released.

**THE WAKEFIELD UNITY HALL**
EMDEE PROMOTIONS PRESENT
**THE DAMNED**
+ SUPPORT
SUNDAY 26th APRIL  DOORS OPEN 7pm
TICKETS £2.50 in advance, £3.00 on door
FROM HMV (BRADFORD), RED RHINO RECORDS (YORK), IMPULSE (SHEFFIELD), JUMBO RECORDS (LEEDS)
OR POSTAL ORDERS AND SAE TO 19/21 SOMERS ST. LEEDS LS1 2RG

THE EXPLOITED
DOGS OF WAR
NEW SINGLE
OUT NOW
SHH 110
SECRET

FREE SEW ON PATCH
AS8502
999
NINE NINE NINE
WITH FIRST 10,000
NEW SINGLE
OBSESSED
From forthcoming album "Concrete"
C/W CHANGE & LIE, LIE, LIE
RELEASE DATE 10th APRIL
999 ON TOUR
APRIL
22 SHEFFIELD TOP RANK
23 WAKEFIELD UNITY HALL
24 EDINBURGH NITE CLUB
25 NOTTINGHAM ROCK CITY
26 CHELTENHAM EVES CLUB
27 MANCHESTER FAGANS
28 LIVERPOOL ROTTERS
29 HUDDERSFIELD EROS CLUB
30 BIRMINGHAM CEDARS
MAY
1 MIDDLESBROUGH TOWN HALL
3 RETFORD PORTERHOUSE
3 LONDON LYCEUM
ION 1011
Distributed by Spartan

**FRIDAY 01 MAY**

The Undertones release the *Positive Touch* LP.

---

**THE OI-BAND**
NEW ALEXANDRA'S WED. 13th MAY
Bath Road, Slough
plus support    plus Alan Gogh's H.M. Roadshow

BOSSARD HALL    FRI. 15th MAY
West Street, Leighton Buzzard
plus support    plus Alan Gogh's H.M. Roadshow

---

**THURSDAY 28 MAY**

The Clash start the first of eight planned shows Bond International Casino in New York City. The venue's legal capacity limit of 1750 is blatantly oversold with twice as many people in attendance.

---

**FRIDAY 22 MAY**

Peter Sutcliffe is sentenced to life imprisonment with a recommendation that he should serve at least 30 years before parole can be considered.

---

**SATURDAY 30 MAY**

The New York City Fire Department cancel the Saturday performance of The Clash at Bond International Casino due to the overcrowding of the venue the previous nights. The band condemn the promoters' greed and respond by doubling the original booking to a total of 17 dates extending through June so that each and every ticketholder gets a chance to see them.

---

**Re-Member**

THE MEMBERS have returned from a lengthy period of 'recuperation' following their dismissal from Virgin. In fact the band have been writing new songs and touring abroad.

They are back as a seven-piece with the original band plus horn players Steve 'Rudy' Thompson and Adam Maithland plus an 'occasional' percussionist when they feel like it.

They've signed a one-off deal with Albion and release a single called 'Working Girl' this week. They also have a series of gigs lined up at Liverpool Brady's May 16, Hammersmith Odeon (with XTC) 21, West Runton Pavilion 22, Retford Porterhouse 23, Birmingham Odeon 24 (with XTC), Rickmansworth Watersmeet 29, Canterbury Kent University June 7. More dates are being set up.

**SATURDAY**

# 13

**JUNE**

Marcus Sarjeant fires six blank cartridges at The Queen as she enters Horse Guards Parade.

1More than 80 arrests are made during clashes between white power skinheads and black people in Coventry, where the National Front is planning a march later this month, on the same day as an anti-racist concert by The Specials.

It's also announced that Ian Dury and The Blockheads will celebrate the upcoming Royal wedding of Prince Charles and Lady Diana Spencer with a special concert at London's Hammersmith Odeon.

**THURSDAY**

# 02

**JULY**

Four members of an Asian Muslim family (three of them children) are killed by arson at their home in Walthamstow, London; the attack is believed to have been racially motivated.

**FRIDAY**

# 03

**JULY**

The Hambrough Tavern public house in Southall, London is set on fire when skinhead group the 4 Skins are booked to appear in the predominantly Asian area. Trouble flares between the Skinheads and the local population that results in a paraffin bomb attack destroying the pub.

**SUNDAY**

# 05

**JULY**

Toxteth riots break out in Liverpool and first use is made of CS gas by British police. Less serious riots occur in the Handsworth district of Birmingham as well as Wolverhampton city centre, parts of Coventry, Leicester and Derby, and also in the Buckinghamshire town High Wycombe.

**TUESDAY**
**07**
JULY

43 people are charged with theft and violent disorder following a riot in Wood Green, North London.

Joe McDonnell becomes the fifth IRA hunger striker to die.

**WEDNESDAY**
**08**
JULY

Inner-city rioting continues when a riot in Moss Side, Manchester, sees more than 1,000 people besiege the local police station. However, the worst rioting in Toxteth has now ended.

After 12 years British Leyland ends production of the Austin Maxi, one of its longest-running cars.

**THURSDAY**
**09**
JULY

Rioting breaks out in Woolwich, London.

Rioting breaks out in London, Birmingham, Leeds, Leicester, Ellesmere Port, Luton, Sheffield, Portsmouth, Preston, Newcastle-upon-Tyne, Derby, Southampton, Nottingham, High Wycombe, Bedford, Edinburgh, Wolverhampton, Stockport, Blackburn, Huddersfield, Reading, Chester and Aldershot.

**FRIDAY**
**10**
JULY

Two days of rioting in Moss Side, Manchester, draw to a close, during which there has been extensive looting of shops. Princess Road, the main road through the area, will be closed for several days while adjacent buildings and gas mains damaged by rioting and arson are made safe.

## Dickie dies after mystery shooting

CHUCK WAGON, (right) keyboards and sax player with The Dickies, is dead. Chuck shot himself at his parents' home in the Valley after getting back from a gig with the band. He died the next night in hospital, writes Silvie Simmons in Los Angeles.

The events leading up to the tragedy are still a bit blurred. Apparently Chuck was in an accident in which his car rolled over on the way back from the Dickies' Topanga Corral show at the weekend. He was driven home by the sound man. He went straight upstairs to his bedroom and shot himself in the head with a .22 caliber pistol.

Chuck — real name Bob Davis; the other name was given to him, along with his job, because he was the proud owner of a 1968 Volkswagen which he would use to transport various Dickies — had quit the band a few months ago and was working on his own material in New York. He came back to record the recently completed new Dickies album and to work the clubs with them after they came out of virtual retirement following A&M Records dropping them.

According to guitarist Stan Lee, the band's still in a state of shock and with no idea what their future will be. At least they're going ahead with the release of the album, a record they seem particularly pleased with.

Chuck Wagon's death is both sad and ironic. Among all the cynical, morbid L.A. punks, the Dickies always stood out as a band with a sense of silliness and humour.

## Damned birthday

THE DAMNED have now confirmed their Fifth Anniversary Celebration at London's Lyceum on July 5. They'll be rushing back from their European tour to do the gig and showing a revolutionary new lighting technique which they've been developing with artist Max Lovegrove.

## Solo sub

THE UK SUBS, who've been without a label since the sudden demise of Gem Records, are in the final stages of negotiating a new deal, which they hope to announce next week.

Meanwhile, Charlie Harper releases his second solo single next weekend on Ramkup Records (through Pinnacle). Called 'Freaked', it consists of Charlie and "a bunch of old cronies (but not as old as Charlie)" made up of Tony Collins guitar, Steve Slack bass, Dave Dudley keyboards and Pete Davies drums.

## The living Dead

**THE DEAD KENNEDYS** will visit Britain in October to play five dates at, as yet, unannounced venues.

While the band are over here they will be promoting the September re-release of their Cherry Red single 'Holidays In Cambodia', available on both 7" and 12". As usual it will be available through Rough Trade and Spartan Records.

---

**SATURDAY 11 JULY**

A further wave of rioting breaks out in Bradford, West Yorkshire.

---

**WEDNESDAY 15 JULY**

Police clash with black youths in Brixton once again, this time after police raid properties in search of petrol bombs which are never found.

---

**WEDNESDAY 29 JULY**

The wedding of Charles, Prince of Wales, and Lady Diana Spencer takes place at St Paul's Cathedral. More than 30 million viewers watch the wedding on television – the second highest British television audience of all time.

---

AUGUST 15. 1981 30p

**THEATRE OF HATE · REDBEAT · CHEFS**
**NEW PSYCHEDELIA**

# sounds

BEKI'S WORKING FOR THE VICE SQUAD p18

VICE SQUAD'S Beki Bondage: pic by Martin Slattery

**MONDAY**

# 24

AUGUST

Mark Chapman is sentenced to 25 years in prison for killing John Lennon.

**FRIDAY 25 SEPTEMBER**

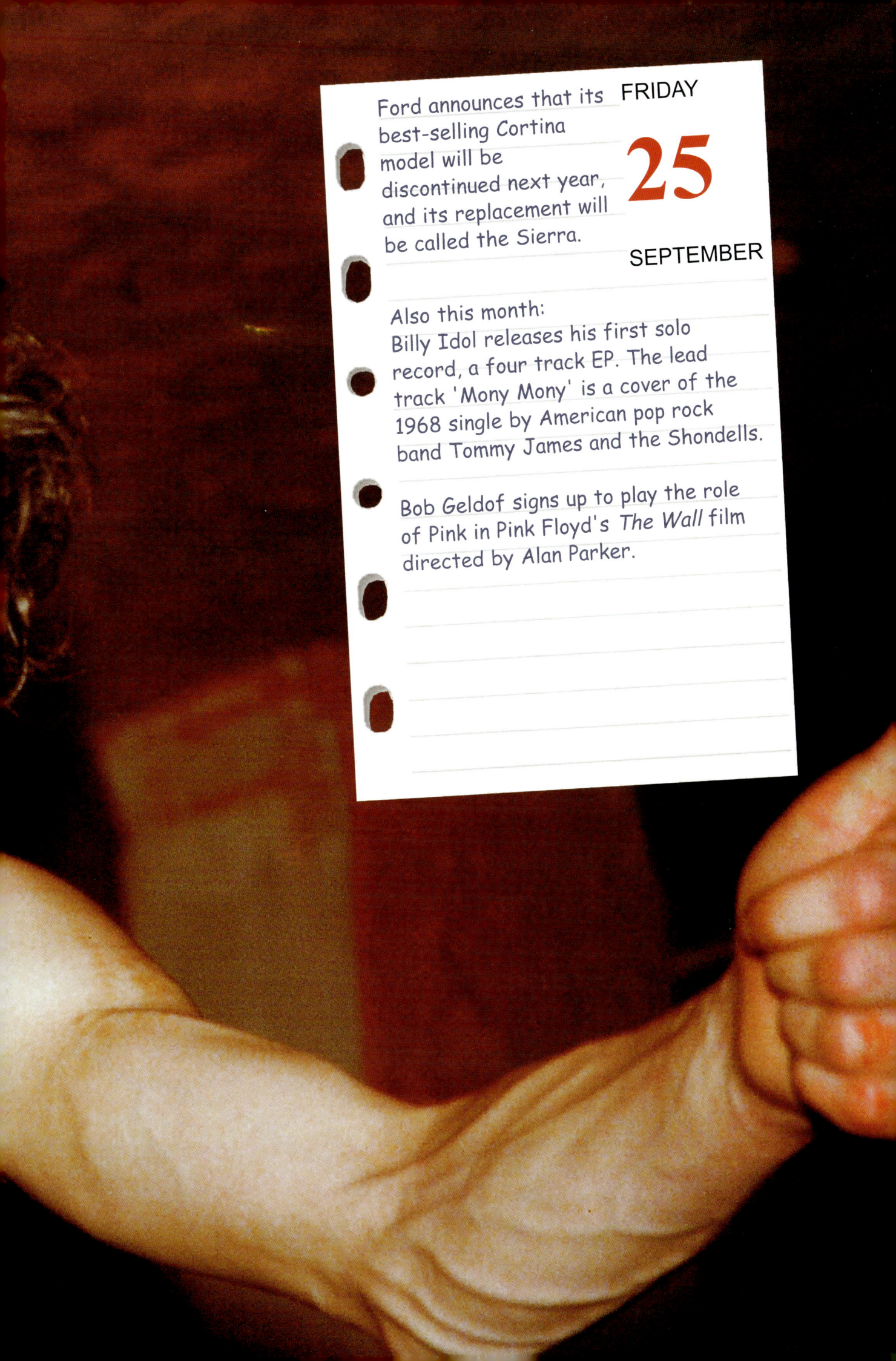

Ford announces that its best-selling Cortina model will be discontinued next year, and its replacement will be called the Sierra.

Also this month:
Billy Idol releases his first solo record, a four track EP. The lead track 'Mony Mony' is a cover of the 1968 single by American pop rock band Tommy James and the Shondells.

Bob Geldof signs up to play the role of Pink in Pink Floyd's *The Wall* film directed by Alan Parker.

**MONDAY**

**12**

**OCTOBER**

British Leyland announces the closure of three factories – a move which will cost nearly 3,000 jobs.

Also this month:
Malcolm McLaren's Bow Wow Wow release *See Jungle! See Jungle! Go Join Your Gang Yeah, City All Over! Go Ape Crazy!*

## Jobson's break

RICHARD JOBSON, lead singer with **The Skids** and more recently, actor and poet, takes a short break from preparing for **The New Skids** first major British tour by undertaking a series of appearances at universities aimed at promoting 'The Ballad Of Etiquette', Richard's album of poetry.

It features Richard reading accompanies by musicians **Virginia** (flute/piano), **Josephine** (soprana sax, clarinet and piano) and **John McGeogh** (guitar).

Richard will be appearing at the venues detailed below with a similar line-up. 'The Ballad Of Etiquette' album is an aural version of Richard's recently published book of poetry, 'A Man For All Seasons'. The book contained Richard's own poetry, while 'The Ballad Of Etiquette' sees him reading the works of other poets.

Dates are: Uxbridge, Brunel University, October 19, Colchester, Essex University, 20, Reading, Reading University, 21, London, City University, 22, Middlesex Polytechnic, 23, (Two shows, lunchtime and evening); Norwich, East Anglia University, 24, Leicester, Leicester University, 26, Stoke-on-Trent, Keele University, 27, Nottingham University, 28, Durham, Durham University, 29, Newcastle, Newcastle University, 30.

Meanwhile, Richard, Russell Webb and the first new member of The Skids, Paul Wishart, are preparing a British tour aimed at supporting the release of their new album 'Joy', which is set for release on November 20.

Their new single, 'Iona'/'Blood And Soil' is released on November 11.

## Stranglers

THE STRANGLERS release their new LP on November 9, entitled 'La Folie'. This will be the band's seventh album and is considered their most commercial for some time.

'La Folie' was recorded recently at the Manor. It was produced by the **Stranglers** and mixed by Tony Visconti.

A single, 'Let Me Introduce You To The Family', will be released on November 2.

The band's forthcoming tour dates are: Norwich, University, November 14, Birmingham, Odeon, 15, Cardiff, Sophia Gardens, 16, London, Hammersmith Palais, 17, Southampton, Gaumont, 19, Nottingham, Rock City, 20, Edinburgh, Playhouse, 22, Glasgow, Apollo, 23, Newcastle, City Hall, 24, Manchester, Apollo, 25, Liverpool, Royal Court Theatre, 26.

## Jam dates

THE JAM have lined up four London dates in December. They'll play two nights at the Michael Sobell Sports Centre in Islington on December 12 and 13 followed by the Hammersmith Palais on the 14th and 15th.

Tickets are £4.50 and available by post only from MCP (to whom you should make cheques and postal orders payable to), PO Box 124, Walsall, West Midlands WS5 4AP. Allow at least a fortnight for processing and don't forget the sae.

The **Jam**'s new single 'Absolute Beginners' is released by Polydor this week but there's no sign of an album to follow at the moment although one is certainly on the way.

## Changes

ANGELIC UPSTARTS have made a few changes to their tour which now runs as follows: Gillingham King Charles Hotel October 15, Birmingham Cedar Ballroom 17, Bristol Granary 19, Derby Rainbow 20, Edinburgh University 21.

---

SUNDAY

**01**

British Leyland's 58,000-strong workforce begins a strike over pay.

NOVEMBER

Also this month:

Paul Weller is booked to read in this month's London Poetry Olympics.

**TUESDAY**

**08**

Arthur Scargill becomes leader of the National Union of Mineworkers.

**DECEMBER**

Also this month:

In God We Trust, Inc. EP is released by the Dead Kennedys.